05-198

D0820338

Genetic Engineering

OPPOSING VIEWPOINTS®

Genetic Engineering

OPPOSING VIEWPOINTS®

Other Books of Related Interest

Genetic Engineering

OPPOSING VIEWPOINTS®

Louise I. Gerdes, *Book Editor*

Bruce Glassman, *Vice President*
Bonnie Szumski, *Publisher*
Helen Cothran, *Managing Editor*

San Diego • Detroit • New York • San Francisco • Cleveland
New Haven, Conn. • Waterville, Maine • London • Munich

For more information, contact
Greenhaven Press
27500 Drake Rd.
Farmington Hills, MI 48331-3535
Or you can visit our Internet site at http://www.gale.com

Cover credit: © PhotoDisc

LIBRARY OF CONGRESS CATALOGING-IN-PUBLICATION DATA
Genetic engineering : opposing viewpoints / Louise I. Gerdes, book editor.
p. cm. — (Opposing viewpoints series)
Includes bibliographical references and index.
ISBN 0-7377-2236-3 (lib. bdg. : alk. paper) —
ISBN 0-7377-2237-1 (pbk. : alk. paper)
1. Genetic engineering—Social aspects. 2. Genetic engineering—Moral and ethical aspects. I. Gerdes, Louise I., 1953– . II. Opposing viewpoints series (Unnumbered)
QH438.7.G413 2004
306.4'6—dc22   2004043660

Printed in the United States of America

"Congress shall make no law. . . abridging the freedom of speech, or of the press."

First Amendment to the U.S. Constitution

The basic foundation of our democracy is the First Amendment guarantee of freedom of expression. The Opposing Viewpoints Series is dedicated to the concept of this basic freedom and the idea that it is more important to practice it than to enshrine it.

Contents

Why Consider
Opposing Viewpoints?

"The only way in which a human being can make some approach to knowing the whole of a subject is by hearing what can be said about it by persons of every variety of opinion and studying all modes in which it can be looked at by every character of mind. No wise man ever acquired his wisdom in any mode but this."

John Stuart Mill

In our media-intensive culture it is not difficult to find differing opinions. Thousands of newspapers and magazines and dozens of radio and television talk shows resound with differing points of view. The difficulty lies in deciding which opinion to agree with and which "experts" seem the most credible. The more inundated we become with differing opinions and claims, the more essential it is to hone critical reading and thinking skills to evaluate these ideas. Opposing Viewpoints books address this problem directly by presenting stimulating debates that can be used to enhance and teach these skills. The varied opinions contained in each book examine many different aspects of a single issue. While examining these conveniently edited opposing views, readers can develop critical thinking skills such as the ability to compare and contrast authors' credibility, facts, argumentation styles, use of persuasive techniques, and other stylistic tools. In short, the Opposing Viewpoints Series is an ideal way to attain the higher-level thinking and reading skills so essential in a culture of diverse and contradictory opinions.

In addition to providing a tool for critical thinking, Opposing Viewpoints books challenge readers to question their own strongly held opinions and assumptions. Most people form their opinions on the basis of upbringing, peer pressure, and personal, cultural, or professional bias. By reading carefully balanced opposing views, readers must directly confront new ideas as well as the opinions of those with whom they disagree. This is not to simplistically argue that everyone who reads opposing views will—or should—change his or her opinion. Instead, the series enhances readers' understanding of their own views by encouraging confrontation with opposing ideas. Careful examination of others' views can lead to the readers' understanding of the logical inconsistencies in their own opinions, perspective on why they hold an opinion, and the consideration of the possibility that their opinion requires further evaluation.

Evaluating Other Opinions

To ensure that this type of examination occurs, Opposing Viewpoints books present all types of opinions. Prominent spokespeople on different sides of each issue as well as well-known professionals from many disciplines challenge the reader. An additional goal of the series is to provide a forum for other, less known, or even unpopular viewpoints. The opinion of an ordinary person who has had to make the decision to cut off life support from a terminally ill relative, for example, may be just as valuable and provide just as much insight as a medical ethicist's professional opinion. The editors have two additional purposes in including these less known views. One, the editors encourage readers to respect others' opinions—even when not enhanced by professional credibility. It is only by reading or listening to and objectively evaluating others' ideas that one can determine whether they are worthy of consideration. Two, the inclusion of such viewpoints encourages the important critical thinking skill of objectively evaluating an author's credentials and bias. This evaluation will illuminate an author's reasons for taking a particular stance on an issue and will aid in readers' evaluation of the author's ideas.

It is our hope that these books will give readers a deeper understanding of the issues debated and an appreciation of the complexity of even seemingly simple issues when good and honest people disagree. This awareness is particularly important in a democratic society such as ours in which people enter into public debate to determine the common good. Those with whom one disagrees should not be regarded as enemies but rather as people whose views deserve careful examination and may shed light on one's own.

Thomas Jefferson once said that "difference of opinion leads to inquiry, and inquiry to truth." Jefferson, a broadly educated man, argued that "if a nation expects to be ignorant and free . . . it expects what never was and never will be." As individuals and as a nation, it is imperative that we consider the opinions of others and examine them with skill and discernment. The Opposing Viewpoints Series is intended to help readers achieve this goal.

David L. Bender and Bruno Leone,
Founders

Greenhaven Press anthologies primarily consist of previously published material taken from a variety of sources, including periodicals, books, scholarly journals, newspapers, government documents, and position papers from private and public organizations. These original sources are often edited for length and to ensure their accessibility for a young adult audience. The anthology editors also change the original titles of these works in order to clearly present the main thesis of each viewpoint and to explicitly indicate the opinion presented in the viewpoint. These alterations are made in consideration of both the reading and comprehension levels of a young adult audience. Every effort is made to ensure that Greenhaven Press accurately reflects the original intent of the authors included in this anthology.

Introduction

"It is hard to imagine what human life will be like even a hundred years from now, but I suspect that the reworking of our own biology will figure heavily in our future."

—Gregory Stock, director of the Program on Medicine, Technology, and Society at the University of California, Los Angeles, School of Public Health

In the early 1970s scientists developed the fundamental techniques of recombinant DNA technology—the artificial addition, deletion, or rearrangement of genetic sequences in order to alter the form and function of an organism. The resulting technologies, known as genetic engineering (GE), include gene therapy, which aims to replace defective genes with healthy genes; gene splicing, which involves the genetic modification of crops by inserting the genetic material of a natural insecticide or vitamins; and cloning, the production of identical genetic copies, which is often used to create the genetic material needed for the other techniques. Almost immediately after these technologies were introduced, some analysts began to voice their fears about potential abuses.

Hoping to calm public fears and thus, some analysts claim, prevent restrictions on their research, in 1975 scientists held a conference at the Asilomar Center in California. Science historian Susan P. Wright claims, "Asilomar was about fashioning a set of beliefs for the American people and their representatives in Congress that would allow scientists to pursue genetic engineering under a system of self-governance." The scientists assured the public that genetic engineering was under control, Wright maintains, and proclaimed that, "the fruits of genetic engineering would benefit everyone." Despite these initial efforts by scientists to alleviate the public's fears, opponents of genetic engineering continue to question the safety and the ethical and social implications of genetic engineering technology. Some commentators note that because the concepts and technical vocabulary used in the genetic engineering field are difficult for nonscientists to understand, those on both sides of the debate manipulate language to misrepresent the nature of the technology. According to columnist and former congressman Jack Kemp, "Solid scientific evidence has been all too lacking in this debate—a war of words and slogans, not ideas and initiatives."

The war of words begins with the definition of genetic engineering. Some scientists claim that genetic engineering is a form of biotechnology—the use of biological processes to solve problems or make useful products. Thus, they assert, genetic engineering is not "new" because farmers some ten thousand years ago used biotechnology to domesticate wild plant species by selecting seeds for cultivation. People have also long been involved in selectively breeding animals, they note. However, molecular biologist Michael Antoniou contends that this definition is misleading:

> The proponents of the use of GE in agriculture argue that mankind has been selecting and manipulating plant and animal food stocks for millennia and that this new technology is simply the next stage in this process. . . . [However] GE employs totally artificial units of genetic material, which are introduced into plant and animal cells using chemical, mechanical or bacterial methods. . . . Clearly these procedures are worlds apart when compared to cross fertilisation between closely related species.

Genetic engineering's opponents also claim that scientists obscure the truth about genetic engineering by using terms that minimize the life on which they are experimenting, particularly when discussing therapeutic cloning, which uses embryonic stem cells—the cells that exist before they differentiate into body tissue cells—to replace defective cells in patients with genetic diseases. According to Kerby Anderson, columnist and national director of Probe Ministries, "The debate about cloning and stem cells is not only a debate about the issues but a war of words where words and concepts are redefined." Anderson maintains, for example, "A human embryo is merely called a blastocyst. Though a correct biological term, it is used to diminish the humanity of the unborn." Anderson also argues that the term "therapeutic cloning," with its shift of focus away from the embryo used in the research and onto those suffering from disease, was introduced by procloning advocates to make cloning more acceptable. He says, "In the stem cell debate, it was

HARSH

disturbing to see how much attention was given to those who might potentially benefit from the research and how little attention was given to the reality that human beings would be destroyed to pursue the research."

Those who support genetic engineering claim that anti–genetic engineering activists use language to inflame the public and misrepresent the true nature of genetic engineering and biomedical research. New Zealand Libertarian Party leader Peter Cresswell asserts, for example, that "technology's attackers litter their statements with arbitrary attacks full of 'might be,' 'could-be,' and 'could-lead-to'—observe how often you hear the speculative words 'may,' 'might,' and 'perhaps' in the anti-GE literature."

Another rhetorical method anti–genetic engineering activists use is to draw analogies from science fiction. Robert W. Tracinski, editor of the objectivist journal *Intellectual Activist*, points to the oft-cited reference to Mary Shelley's *Frankenstein*:

Social issue!

> The common theme of these literary works is that too much science and technology—too much human control over nature—is dangerous. . . . Just as Mary Shelley's mad scientist warns, "learn from . . . my example how dangerous is the acquirement of knowledge, and how [miserable is] he who aspires to become greater than his nature will allow"—so Leon Kass, a University of Chicago professor and "medical ethicist," warns against "the Frankensteinian hubris to create human life and increasingly to control its destiny, man playing at being God."

By using fiction to warn of the imagined horrors of genetic engineering and the inhumanity of genetic scientists, argues Tracinski, genetic engineering opponents need not point to any real dangers.

Despite pleas for reasoned public debate, the war of words in the genetic engineering debate continues. The authors in *Opposing Viewpoints: Genetic Engineering* share their views about the risks and benefits of genetic engineering in the following chapters: How Will Genetic Engineering Affect Society? Is Genetic Engineering Ethical? What Is the Impact of Genetically Engineered Crops? How Should Genetic Engineering Be Regulated? Those who lead the genetic engineering debate use words not only to facilitate the public's understanding of genetic engineering technology but also to influence people's attitudes toward these technologies. Lee M. Silver, professor of molecular biology and public affairs at Princeton University, concludes, "With the political debate at fever pitch . . . it will come down to an argument over words, not biology."

CHAPTER 1

How Will Genetic Engineering Affect Society?

Chapter Preface

The impact that germ-line gene therapy will have on society is controversial. Germ-line cells are reproductive cells—sperm or eggs. Germ-line gene therapy, also known as human inheritable genetic modification (IGM), involves the insertion of healthy genes into these germ cells to create a beneficial genetic change—such as eliminating a genetic disease—before a child is born. Some believe society will benefit from germ-line gene therapy because debilitating and life-threatening genetic diseases could be eradicated by such therapies. Others fear that the technology will be abused, and humanity will become divided between the genetic haves and the genetic have-nots.

Although scientists have not yet perfected germ-line gene therapy nor performed sanctioned experiments on human subjects, some commentators envision a terrifying future. Journalist Sally Deneen paints a frightening picture:

> It will start innocently enough: Birth defects that are caused by a single gene, such as cystic fibrosis and Tay-Sachs disease, will be targeted first, and probably with little controversy. Then, as societal fears about messing with Mother Nature subside, . . . a genetic solution to preventing diabetes, heart disease and other big killers will be found and offered. So will genetic inoculations against HIV. Eventually, the mind will be targeted for improvement—preventing alcohol addiction and mental illness, and enhancing visual acuity or intelligence to try to produce the next Vincent Van Gogh or Albert Einstein. Even traits from other animals may be added, such as a dog's sense of smell or an eagle's eyesight. What parents would see as a simple, if pricey, way to improve their kids would result, after many generations of gene selection, in a profound change by the year 2400—humans would be two distinct species, related as humans and chimps are today, and just as unable to interbreed.

While some critics concede that this picture is far-fetched, they do fear that those who cannot afford germ-line gene therapy will eventually become second-class citizens. According to Jesse Reynolds, program director for the Center for Genetics and Society, "Applications such as IGM and human reproductive cloning should be opposed because they undermine fundamental norms of equality and will have terrible social consequences." Like-minded critics contend, for example, that while germ-line gene therapy to eliminate disease might be covered by health insurance, such therapy used for genetic enhancement—to design the child of your choice by selecting desirable traits—would not; thus only the rich could afford these "designer" children. Donald Bruce, director of the Church of Scotland's Project on Science and Technology, claims that Great Britain's national health insurance program, which provides near universal access to medical services, would not likely pay for genetic enhancement. Thus, Bruce reasons, "what you've got is the rich hard-wiring their economic and social advantages using genetics."

Other commentators assert that germ-line gene therapy would benefit society because the procedure holds the potential to stamp out many genetic diseases. British philosopher John Harris argues, "If creating a world with less disability and disease seems preferable, then, like me, you will believe in minimizing disease and disability and maximizing health and good fortune." In answer to the argument that selecting characteristics through germ-line gene therapy will create inequality, Harris reasons, "Normal sexual reproduction has always had a large element of design in it. Cultures, religions and races that have encouraged their members to marry other members of the same group are all into designer children."

Whether germ-line gene therapy will be used to eradicate genetic diseases or divide humanity remains a controversial topic that the authors in the following chapter explore. They also examine other controversies surrounding the likely impact that genetic engineering will have on society.

"So powerful is [genetic engineering] technology that literally tens of millions of lives worldwide have been protected, enriched, and even lengthened."

Genetic Engineering Benefits Society

Henry I. Miller and Gregory Conko

The medicines and foods that have been created with the help of modern biotechnology—also known as genetic engineering—benefit millions of people worldwide, claim Henry I. Miller and Gregory Conko in the following viewpoint. Modern gene-splicing techniques, the authors maintain, have resulted in life-saving medicines and improvements in agriculture. Unfortunately, they argue, unfounded accusations that genetically engineered products threaten children's health discourage the use of products that could actually save children's lives. Miller is a research fellow at the Hoover Institution, a Stanford university think tank, and Conko is director of food safety policy at the Competitive Enterprise Institute, a public policy organization dedicated to free enterprise and limited government.

use questions in paper

As you read, consider the following questions:

1. According to the authors, why do scare campaigns focus on attacking agricultural applications of biotechnology?
2. In the authors' opinion, what are some of the nutritional benefits gene-spliced plants could deliver to people in less developed nations?
3. What is the antibiotechnology "kid" campaign likely to exacerbate, in the authors' view?

Henry I. Miller and Gregory Conko, "Biotech and Baby Food," *Policy Review*, June/July 2003, pp. 45–57. Copyright © 2003 by The Heritage Foundation. Reproduced by permission.

Warnings about one societal danger or another often portray children as the likeliest or most susceptible victims. As is the case with so many other public health false alarms, the attack on the new biotechnology—also known as bioengineering, gene splicing, or genetic engineering—is less about real concern for children's health than about environmental activists' willingness to exploit children's issues for their own benefit. Biotechnology has been the target of scare campaigns since the technique was first demonstrated in 1973. Activists, like Jeremy Rifkin of the Foundation on Economic Trends, have been warning against the supposed dangers of biotechnology for three decades, calling it "the most radical, uncontrolled experiment we've ever seen" and even likening it to "Nazi eugenics [the creation of a superior race by eliminating undesirable genetic traits]." Others have claimed that gene-spliced crop plants are "worse than nuclear weapons or radioactive wastes." Fortunately, the American public has not taken such arguments seriously.

The first biotechnology-derived medical treatment, human insulin, was commercialized in 1982, and the first biotech plant in 1994. During the past two decades, thousands of new medicines, foods, and industrial products have been produced with the aid of modern biotechnology and sold to doctors, farmers, manufacturers, and consumers. So powerful is the technology that literally tens of millions of lives worldwide have been protected, enriched, and even lengthened due entirely to these techniques. But so subtle and precise are the production changes generated by the technology that very few people recognize how widely biotechnology figures in everyday life. . . .

How Safe Is Biotechnology?

Although most Americans have not succumbed to the ideological scare-mongering campaign against biotechnology, they cannot avoid hearing over and over about the supposed threats to children's health. Increasingly, some Americans are beginning to view gene-spliced foods with more than a little skepticism. Of course, those who are critical of biotechnology are often unaware of an important, fundamental point: The modification of organisms at the basic genetic level is not new, and consumers, farmers, and industries all have extensive—and positive—experience with it. Even the term "biotechnology" was once used in a much broader sense, to describe any application of biological organisms to technical or industrial processes. A primitive form of food biotechnology dates back at least to 6000 BC when the Babylonians used microorganisms in fermentation to brew alcoholic beverages. Only in recent years has biotechnology come to connote only the most sophisticated methods for modifying organisms at the genetic level.

During the course of the twentieth century, a better understanding of genes and cell biology added to the improvement of all manner of organisms. An excellent example is the genetic modification of *Penicillium chrysogenum*, the mold that produces penicillin. Using a variety of techniques, the mold has been altered to produce more and more penicillin, and yields have increased more than a hundredfold in the past five decades. Similarly, agricultural crops have been genetically improved with astonishing success with both "natural" and "unnatural" breeding techniques. These applications of older biotechnologies represent scientific, technological, commercial, and humanitarian successes of monumental proportions. The "conventional" genetic modification of wheat plants was recognized in 1970 when the Nobel Peace Prize was awarded to Dr. Norman Borlaug, the "Father of the Green Revolution."

The Impact of Modern Technology

However, the techniques used for these earlier successes were relatively crude and recently have been supplemented, and in many cases supplanted, by modern biotechnology. The techniques described by practitioners as gene splicing, genetic engineering, or recombinant DNA engineering use a variety of tools to identify single genes from one organism, isolate and remove them from the surrounding DNA and then insert them into the DNA strands of other organisms. Because the DNA in every living organism is made up of the same basic chemicals—and because DNA works in essentially the same way whether it's in a bacterium, a plant, or an animal—a gene can be moved from one organism to another and still produce the same trait. And the products of modern biotechnology can be used for a variety of purposes—including modified bacteria for cleaning up oil spills; a weakened virus used as a vaccine; a protein, such as insulin, used to treat diabetics; or a crop plant modified to need less pesticides or to be more nutritious.

Dozens of scientific bodies, including the UK's [United Kingdom's] Royal Society, the U.S. National Academy of Sciences, the World Health Organization, and the American Medical Association, have studied modern biotechnology and gene-spliced organisms and arrived at remarkably congruent conclusions about their safety:

• Modern genetic modification techniques are an extension, or refinement, of earlier, far less precise ones;

• Simply adding genes to plants or microorganisms does not make them less safe either for the environment or for humans;

• The risks associated with gene-spliced organisms are the same in kind as those associated with conventionally modified organisms (and in both cases are usually extremely low); and

• Regulation of the products of genetic modification should be based upon the risk-related characteristics of individual products, regardless of whether newer techniques are used in their development.

Thus, the primary thing that has changed since the introduction of gene-splicing methods in the early 1970s is the *technology* of biotechnology. The new technology, however, is more precise and predictable than its predecessors and yields better-characterized and more predictable products. There are already more than 100 gene-spliced medicines on the market and more than 300 more in clinical development. Marketed products include human insulin, used daily by millions of American diabetics; tissue plasminogen activator, a protein that dissolves the blood clots that cause heart attacks and strokes; human growth hormone, used to treat children with hormonal deficiency; erythropoietin, which stimulates the growth of red blood cells in certain patients suffering from anemia and is especially beneficial to cancer patients who have undergone chemotherapy; and several interferons, proteins used to treat a variety of maladies from multiple sclerosis to viral infections and cancer.

The Agricultural Applications

This reality of current therapeutics, along with the vast potential of biotechnology to produce new and better medicines, presents such a powerful argument for the medicinal use of biotechnology that it has been difficult for anti-technology activists to challenge it. Scare campaigns have instead typically focused on attacking agricultural applications of biotechnology. But gene-spliced plants have also shown many important benefits for both farmers and consumers, as well as for the environment.

Dozens of gene-spliced crop and garden plants now on the market have been genetically improved with a range of new traits, including resistance to insect pests and plant diseases. Gene-spliced varieties of insect-resistant corn and cotton have been modified to produce a protein that is toxic to certain chewing insects but not to birds, fish, or mammals, including humans. In turn, they require fewer applications of synthetic pesticides and generate higher yields. Gene-spliced varieties of soybean and canola that are resistant to one or another herbicide allow farmers to spray less and still control weeds effectively. Because this eliminates the need for mechanical cultivation to remove weeds, herbicide-tolerant crop plants protect topsoil from eroding easily, which has been a major agricultural and environmental concern for decades. And biotech-derived growth hormones for livestock, like cows and pigs, can help farmers produce more meat and milk at a lower price and with less nitrogen and phosphorous waste from the animals.

The Tactics of Scaremongers

One such hormone, recombinant bovine somatotropin (rbst), or bovine growth hormone, has been a target of activists for nearly two decades. The Food and Drug Administration approved the product in 1993 to boost milk production in cows after more than 10 years of intensive scrutiny (although, years earlier, the agency had approved the analogous human hormone for use in growth-hormone-deficient children after a mere 18 months of review). But scaremongers have often claimed that administration of the hormone to cows was potentially hazardous to consumers of the milk—

The ABCs of Human Genetic Engineering

If scientists were to begin altering the human genome, a woman's egg would first be removed from her body and fertilized through in vitro fertilization, creating an embryo. The embryo is copied through cloning, and new genes are spliced into each embryo's germline—the genetic blueprint created from the genetic material contained in sperm and egg cells. Each cell in an organism resulting from the embryo will contain the new gene. Any physiological changes caused by the new gene, such as resistance to cancer or increased memory, could be passed on to future generations through normal reproduction.

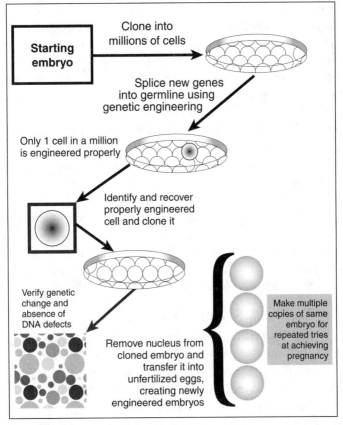

Lee Silver, Princeton University, 2001.

causing, for example, immune deficiencies in children. One activist, Samuel Epstein of the Cancer Prevention Coalition, has charged that drinking milk from cows given rbst will cause an increase in childhood cancers—even though milk from treated cows is chemically indistinguishable from other milk.

But scientific evidence doesn't seem to matter. Activists have targeted schools, day care centers, and even the coffee retail chain Starbucks for boycotts and petition campaigns calling for the end of rbst use, in spite of endorsements for the product by such esteemed scientific bodies as the American Medical Association, the American Cancer Society, the National Institutes of Health, and the United Nations World Health Organization and Food and Agricultural Organization.

The adoption of rbst by U.S. farmers in the face of such antagonism has been remarkable. But it demonstrates an important correlation that exists between citizens' well-being and government policies that encourage product innovation. Farmers use rbst, which increases the productivity of their cows roughly 10 percent to 25 percent. This, in turn, enables them to produce the same amount of milk with fewer expenditures, making the farmers better off and reducing the retail price for consumers. Ultimately, if government agencies were to keep the regulation of research and development only to the level that is necessary and sufficient, the quest for profits would stimulate researchers' and industry's interest in making more products like rbst. . . .

The Promise of Healthier Children

There are plenty of other important health benefits that food biotechnology holds in store. One good example is the addition of vitamins, minerals, and essential amino acids into staples, such as grain crops, that have little micronutrient value. Another is the ongoing research into developing vegetables with higher levels of potentially beneficial micronutrients. Varieties of soybean and canola, which have been modified with modern biotechnology to produce healthier cooking oils with less saturated fat, are even now being grown on tens of thousands of acres in the United States and Canada.

Even more important are the nutritional benefits that gene-spliced plants could deliver to people in less developed nations. For example, the diet of more than 200 million children worldwide includes inadequate levels of many important micronutrients such as vitamin A. In Asia, this is often caused by the weaning of poor children on little more than rice gruel. Deficiency in this single micronutrient can result in impaired intellectual development, blindness, and even death; each year, approximately 2 million children die from a severe lack of vitamin A. Fortunately, a substantial amount of research into improving the nutritional value of staple crops is well underway. Perhaps the most promising . . . advance in this area is the development of a rice variety that has been genetically enhanced to add beta carotene into the edible grains, which is then converted in the human body to vitamin A. It is estimated that by boosting the availability of vitamin A in developing-world diets, this variety, called Golden Rice, could help prevent as many as a million deaths per year and eliminate numerous other health problems. A similar modification to increase iron content is also under active investigation.

And there are many other ways in which biotechnology can help poor women and children, who perform much of the daily farm work in less developed countries. One approach is to enhance the ability of many kinds of crop plants to grow in poor soils, a problem that reduces cereal crop productivity over vast areas of the earth, but primarily in the poorer nations of the tropical zone. Adding genes to rice and corn that enable the plants to tolerate high concentrations of aluminum in the soil is the goal of a team of scientists in Mexico. Other researchers, at the University of Toronto and the University of California at Davis, are creating crop varieties that can be irrigated with poor quality, brackish water. And there are many similar examples of crop modifications, such as improving the ability of plants to grow in alkaline, iron-poor soil, that could have direct and substantial benefits for poor farmers.

The Value of Gene Splicing

Gene splicing can also address the monumental need in less developed countries for both new childhood vaccines and cheaper versions of existing vaccines. The latter can be achieved by lowering production costs and/or reducing the cost of immunization—for example, by eliminating the need for refrigeration or developing oral vaccines that do not require a needle and syringe. Gene-spliced plants are already being developed that contain edible vaccines against many infectious scourges rampant in developing nations, including hepatitis B and various diarrheal diseases.

Even currently marketed gene-spliced products, such as the pest-resistant cotton so popular in the United States, have permitted farmers in less developed nations such as South Africa and China to reduce their dependence on synthetic pesticides. Cotton farming uses very large doses of pesticides, and in less developed nations those pesticides are typically sprayed on crops by hand. This is often labor-intensive and expensive. In addition, in China, for example, some 400 to 500 farm workers die every year from acute pesticide poisoning, and approximately 50,000, many of them women and children, have suffered serious illnesses since 1987, attributed to on-farm contact with pesticides. But the introduction of gene-spliced, pest-resistant cotton varieties in China has reduced pesticide poisonings by nearly 80 percent among growers of the biotech varieties.

While plant geneticists are working to engineer many useful traits into crop plants, some of the benefits of biotechnology will be wholly unanticipated. Consider again the pest-resistant corn example described above. That gene-spliced variety has been found to reduce considerably the levels of harmful fumonisin [a common toxin and contaminant in corn and other cereals] toxins in harvested grains, an important, although poorly appreciated, health benefit. In industrialized countries like the United States and Canada, strict processing standards and sophisticated testing methods keep the amounts of fumonisin in food well below dangerous levels. But in poorer regions of the world, where corn is usually grown in small plots by single families who consume most or all of the produce, such quality control is nonexistent.

In 1990 and 1991, the number of babies born in and around the south Texas town of Brownsville with an extraordinarily rare condition called anencephaly—in which the brain of the newborn infant is stunted or missing—rose to double the normal rate, then returned to normal the following year. The condition was found primarily among the children of poor Mexican immigrant mothers, who tend to consume very large amounts of corn every day in tortillas alone. After initially suspecting industrial pollutants as the culprit, the Texas Department of Health now blames the near-epidemic on exceptionally high fumonisin levels in corn caused by a multi-year drought in northern Mexico and the southwestern United States. Similar examples undoubtedly occur without documentation throughout the world. But biotech products like pest-resistant corn could be an important way to reduce the incidence of such heart-rending problems.

Creating Unwarranted Fear

Even such desperately needed biotech products as these do not escape the activist scare campaigns. When the United States Agency for International Development sent a shipment of corn and soy meal to aid the victims of a cyclone in the Indian province of Orissa, anti-technology activists took samples of the food to test whether or not it contained gene–spliced varieties. When they found that it did, Vandana Shiva, director of the New Delhi-based Research Foundation for Science, Technology and Ecology, an environmental activist group, argued: "The U.S. has been using the Orissa victims as guinea pigs for [gene-spliced] products"—even though these were the very same biotech corn and soy varieties that U.S. consumers had been eating for years.

To biotechnology critics like *New York Times Magazine* food journalist Michael Pollan, Golden Rice is just a "Great Yellow Hype"—a ploy by multinational biotechnology corporations to get the world hooked on gene splicing. Never mind that the research was funded primarily by the New York-based Rockefeller Foundation, which has promised to make the rice available to developing-world farmers at little or no cost. Is-mail Serageldin, director of the UN-sponsored Consultative Group on International Agricultural Research, asks biotech opponents: "Do you want two to three million children a year to go blind and one million to die of vitamin A deficiency, just because you object to the way golden rice was created?" Apparently, in their opposition to biotechnology, critics find it more important to use children as a symbol than actually to make the world a safer or healthier place for kids.

In spite of significant and real—not merely conjectural— benefits of gene-spliced foods, the anti-biotechnology "kid campaign" has borne fruit for environmentalists in a way that other forms of activism could not. Whether the campaign will ever succeed in frightening large numbers of American consumers away from biotech is yet to be seen. It is, however, likely to exacerbate the tendency of governments to over-regulate modern genetic technologies. The activists need not scare consumers or food processors completely to succeed in destroying biotechnology. They could be successful simply by weakening public support just enough to provoke unnec-essary and poorly conceived legislation or regulation.

Already, most regulatory agencies have treated gene-spliced foods and crop plants in a discriminatory, unnecessar-ily burdensome way. They have imposed costly and time-consuming requirements that could not possibly be met for conventionally bred plants. Agricultural biotechnology re-search and development have become so expensive that re-search on developing countries' subsistence crops—millet, cassava, sorghum, yams, and the like—has almost evaporated. Research on tropical rice varieties has continued only cour-tesy of huge subsidies from governments and charities, such as the Rockefeller Foundation. Adding still more regulation could turn gene splicing into a kind of boutique technology that is applied primarily to high-value products that are af-fordable only by the affluent. The biggest losers would be the inhabitants of less developed countries and lower-income consumers everywhere else. Thus, the safe and effective products of this technology, which hold so much promise for improving the health of children, could be stripped from their hands by a campaign perversely designed to exploit them for political gain.

"Genetic engineering poses . . . serious challenges to the environment, human health, animal welfare, and the future of agriculture."

Genetic Engineering Threatens Society

Ronnie Cummins

In the following viewpoint Ronnie Cummins argues that genetic engineering poses many threats to society. Cummins claims, for example, that living things will be reduced to commodities because biotech corporations will hold patents on genes and genetically engineered products, making them "owners" of engineered organisms. Moreover, he asserts, because genetically engineered foods will eventually be produced in factories, not farms, millions of farmers worldwide will lose their livelihoods. He also maintains that widespread genetic screening of human embryos, the objective of which is to abort embryos with genetic diseases and undesirable traits, could lead to discrimination against genetically "inferior" people. Cummins, executive director of the Organic Consumers Association, is author of *Genetically Engineered Food: A Self-Defense Guide for Consumers.*

As you read, consider the following questions:

1. In Cummins's opinion, why do "biological pollutants" have the potential to be even more destructive than chemical pollutants?
2. According to Cummins, what are some of the biological weapons the U.S. military is developing?

G enetic engineering is a radical new technology, one that
breaks down fundamental genetic barriers—not only
between species, but also between humans, animals, and
plants. By combining the genes of dissimilar and unrelated
species, permanently altering their genetic codes, novel organisms are created that will pass the genetic changes onto
their offspring through heredity. Scientists are now snipping,
inserting, recombining, rearranging, editing, and program-
ming genetic material. Animal genes and even human genes
are being inserted into plants or animals creating unimagined
transgenic life forms. For the first time in history, human beings are becoming the architects of life. Bio-engineers will be
creating tens of thousands of novel organisms over the next
few years. As of August 1998 no less than 37 genetically engineered foods and crops have been approved for commer-
cialization in the US—with absolutely no pre-market safety
testing or labeling required. The prospect, or rather the reality, of the Biotech Century that lies ahead is frightening.

Genetic engineering poses unprecedented ethical and social concerns, as well as serious challenges to the environment, human health, animal welfare, and the future of agriculture. The following is just a sampling of concerns:

The Threats to the Environment

Genetically engineered organisms that escape or are released from the laboratory can wreak environmental havoc.

Genetically engineered "biological pollutants" have the
potential to be even more destructive than chemical pollutants. Because they are alive, genetically engineered products
can reproduce, migrate, and mutate. Once released, it will be
virtually impossible to recall genetically engineered organisms. A report published by 100 top American scientists
warned that the release of gene-spliced organisms ". . . could
lead to irreversible, devastating damage to the ecology."

Genetically engineered products do not have a good track
record for human safety. In 1989 and 1990, a genetically engineered brand of L-tryptophan, a common dietary supplement, killed more than 30 Americans and permanently dis-
abled or afflicted more than 1,500 others with a potentially
fatal and painful blood disorder, eosinophilia myalgia syn-

drome, before it was recalled by the FDA. The manufacturer, Showa Denko K.K., Japan's third largest chemical company, had used genetically engineered bacteria to produce the over-the-counter supplement. It is believed that the bacteria somehow became contaminated during the recombinant DNA process. There were no labels to identify the product as having been genetically engineered.

Changing the Nature of Farming

The patenting of genetically engineered foods, and widespread biotech food production, will eliminate farming as it has been practiced since the beginning. If the trend is not stopped, the patenting of transgenic plants and food-producing animals will soon lead to tenant farming in which farmers will lease their plants and animals from biotech conglomerates and pay royalties on seeds and offspring. Eventually, within the next few decades, agriculture will move off the soil and into biosynthetic industrial factories controlled by chemical and biotech companies. Never again will people know the joy of eating naturally produced fresh foods. Hundreds of millions of farmers and other workers worldwide will lose their livelihoods. The hope of creating a human, sustainable agricultural system will be destroyed.

The genetic engineering and patenting of animals reduces living beings to the status of manufactured products and will result in much suffering. In January 1994, then-USDA [U.S. Department of Agriculture] Secretary Mike Espy announced that USDA scientists had completed genome "road maps" for cattle and pigs, a precursor to ever more experimentation on live animals. In addition to the cruelty inherent in such experimentation (the mistakes are born with painful deformities, crippled, blind, and so on), these "manufactured" creatures have no greater value to their "creators" than mechanical inventions. Animals genetically engineered for use in laboratories, such as the infamous "Harvard mouse" which contains a human cancer-causing gene that will be passed down to all succeeding generations, were created to suffer.

A purely reductionist science, biotechnology reduces all life to bits of information (genetic code) that can be arranged and rearranged at whim. Stripped of their integrity and sacred qualities, animals that are merely objects to their "inventors" will be treated as such. Currently, more than 200 genetically engineered "freak" animals are awaiting patent approval from the federal government.

An Unregulated Industry

No one is regulating genetically engineered organisms adequately or properly testing them for safety. In 1986, Reagan-era policymakers stitched together a patchwork of preexisting and only marginally appropriate statutes to ease the way for new biotechnology products. But these laws were created years ago to deal with chemicals—not the unpredictable living products of genetic engineering. To date, no suitable government apparatus has been set up to deal with this radical new class of potentially overwhelming environmental and health threats.

The FDA's policy on genetically altered foods illustrates the problem. In May 1992, then Vice President Dan Quayle, head of the Competitiveness Council, announced the US Food and Drug Administration's newly developed policy on biotech foods: genetically engineered foods will not be treated differently from naturally produced foods; they will not be safety tested; they will not carry labels stating that they have been genetically engineered, nor will the government keep track of foods that have been genetically engineered. As a result, neither the government nor consumers will know which whole or processed foods have been genetically engineered.

Vegetarians and followers of religious dietary restrictions face the prospect of unwittingly eating vegetables and fruits that contain genetic material from animals—including humans. And health risks will be discovered only by trial and error—by consumers. USDA oversight is no better. This agency has the conflicting task of both promoting and regulating agriculture, including genetically engineered plants and animals used for food. Indeed, the USDA is a primary sponsor of biotech research on plants and animals.

Controlling the Blueprint of Life

By patenting the genes they discover and the living organisms they create, a small corporate elite will soon own and

The Genetic Bill of Rights

1. All people have the right to preservation of the earth's biological and genetic diversity.

2. All people have the right to a world in which living organisms cannot be patented, including human beings, animals, plants, microorganisms and all their parts.

3. All people have the right to a food supply that has not been genetically engineered.

4. All indigenous peoples have the right to manage their own biological resources, to preserve their traditional knowledge, and to protect these from expropriation and biopiracy by scientific, corporate or government interests.

5. All people have the right to protection from toxins, other contaminants, or actions that can harm their genetic makeup and that of their offspring.

6. All people have the right to protection against eugenic measures such as forced sterilization or mandatory screening aimed at aborting or manipulating selected embryos or fetuses.

7. All people have the right to genetic privacy including the right to prevent the taking or storing of bodily samples for genetic information without their voluntary informed consent.

8. All people have the right to be free from genetic discrimination.

9. All people have the right to DNA tests to defend themselves in criminal proceedings.

10. All people have the right to have been conceived, gestated, and born without genetic manipulation.

The Council for Responsible Genetics, Spring 2000.

control the genetic heritage of the planet. Scientists who "discover" genes and ways of manipulating them can patent not only genetic engineering techniques, but also the very genes themselves. Chemical, pharmaceutical, and biotech companies such as DuPont, Upjohn, Bayer, Dow, Monsanto, Ciba-Geigy, and Rhone-Poulenc, are urgently trying to identify and patent plant, animal, and human genes in order to complete their take-over of agriculture, animal husbandry, and food processing. These are some of the same companies that once promised a carefree life through pesticides and plastics. Would you trust them with the blueprints of life?

Genetic screening will likely lead to a loss of privacy and new levels of discrimination. Already, people are being denied health insurance on the basis of "faulty" genes. Will employers require genetic screening of their employees and deny them work on the basis of the results? Will the government have access to our personal genetic profiles? One can easily imagine new levels of discrimination being directed against those whose genetic profiles reveal them to be, for example, less intelligent or predisposed to developing certain illnesses.

Genetic engineering is already being used to "improve" the human race, a practice called eugenics. Genetic screening already allows us to identify and abort fetuses that carry genes for certain hereditary disorders. But within the next decade, scientists will likely have a complete map of the human genome to work with. Will we abort fetuses on the basis of non-life-threatening impairments such as myopia, because someone is predisposed towards homosexuality, or for purely cosmetic reasons?

Researchers at the University of Pennsylvania have applied for a patent to genetically alter sperm cells in animals so traits passed down from one generation to the next can be changed; the application suggests that this can be done in humans too. Scientists are now routinely cloning sheep, mice, and soon other animals. Moving from animal eugenics to human eugenics is one small step. Everyone wants the best for their children; but where do we stop? Inadvertently, we could soon make the efforts of the Nazis to create a "superior" race seem bumbling and inefficient.

The US military is building an arsenal of genetically engineered biological weapons. Although the creation of biological weapons for offensive purposes has been outlawed by international treaty, the US continues to develop such weapons for defensive purposes. However, genetically engineered biological agents are identical whether they are used for offensive or defensive purposes. Areas of investigation for such weapons include: bacteria that can resist all antibiotics; extra-hardy, more virulent bacteria and viruses that live longer and kill faster; and new organisms that can defeat vaccines or natural human or plant resistances. Also being studied are the development of pathogens that can disrupt human hormonal balance enough to cause death, and the transformation of innocuous bacteria (such as are found in human intestines) into killers. Some experts believe that genetically engineered pathogens that can target specific racial groups are being developed as well.

Not all scientists are sanguine about genetic engineering. Among the doubters is Erwin Chargoff, the eminent biochemist who is often referred to as the father of molecular biology. He warned that all innovation does not result in "progress." Chargoff once referred to genetic engineering as "a molecular Auschwitz" and warned that the technology of genetic engineering poses a greater threat to the world than the advent of nuclear technology. "I have the feeling that science has transgressed a barrier that should have remained inviolate," he wrote in his autobiography, *Heraclitean Fire*. Noting the "awesome irreversibility" of genetic engineering experiments being planned, Chargoff warned that; ". . . you cannot recall a new form of life . . . It will survive you and your children and your children's children. An irreversible attack on the biosphere is something so unheard-of, so unthinkable to previous generations, that I could only wish that mine had not been guilty of it."

"The cloning of a human raises fundamental questions that go to the very nature of what it means to be a human being."

Human Cloning Will Harm Society

Jeremy Rifkin

According to Jeremy Rifkin in the following viewpoint, human cloning will reduce human life to a commodity. Rifkin argues that ultimately control of reproduction will be taken from individuals and placed in the hands of corporations, which will patent both cloning technology and cloned human embryos. Biotech companies will determine the uses to which cloning will be put, Rifkin claims, which could lead to commercial eugenics—breeding humans to eliminate undesirable genetic traits. Rifkin, president of the Foundation on Economic Trends, is the author of *The Biotech Century: Harnessing the Gene and Remaking the World.*

As you read, consider the following questions:

1. How does Rifkin answer the argument that medical science needs embryonic stem cells for research purposes?
2. Why do most people have an almost instinctual revulsion to cloning, in the author's view?
3. According to Rifkin, what will be one of the seminal political issues of the Biotech Century?

Jeremy Rifkin, "Why I Oppose Human Cloning," *Tikkun*, vol. 17, July/August 2002, pp. 23–26. Copyright © 2002 by the Institute for Labor and Mental Health. Reproduced by permission of Tikkun: A Bimonthly Jewish Critique of Politics, Culture & Society.

The cloning and stem cell debate has been viewed in Washington and the media as a classic Right vs. Left struggle, pitting social conservatives, right-to-life activists, and the Catholic Church against the scientific community and progressive forces, with Republicans lined up on one side and Democrats on the other. In reality, however, many of us in the progressive Left are also opposed to cloning, although our reasons differ in some respects from those of the social conservatives. Earlier [in 2002], sixty-seven leading progressives lent their support to legislation[1] that would outlaw both therapeutic and full-birth (also called reproductive) cloning. The signatories of the anti-cloning petition included many of the best-known intellectuals and activists in left circles today.

While the social conservatives' opposition to cloning is well understood, little or no attention has been given in the media or public debate as to why some of us on the Left oppose cloning. We worry that the market for women's eggs that would be created by this research will provide unethical incentives for women to undergo health-threatening hormone treatment and surgery. We are also concerned about the increasing bio-industrialization of life by the scientific community and life science companies; we are shocked and dismayed that clonal human embryos have been patented and declared to be human "inventions." We oppose efforts to reduce human life and its various parts and processes to the status of mere research tools, manufactured products, and utilities.

Answering the Medical Community

To the argument that medical science needs embryonic stem cells for research purposes, we answer that adult stem cells, which can be taken from individuals after birth, have proved promising in both animal studies and clinical trials. This "soft path" approach to using the new science poses none of

---

1. In February 2003 the House of Representatives passed the Human Cloning Prohibition Act of 2003, which would ban all human cloning, including therapeutic and reproductive cloning. The bill is virtually identical to one that passed the House in 2002, on which the Senate failed to act. The Senate has, as of this writing, not approved the 2003 bill.

the ethical, social, and economic risks of strategies using embryo stem cells.

Moreover, many, if not most, of the diseases researchers hope to cure by using embryonic stem cells are the result of a complex choreography acted out between genetic predispositions and environmental triggers. By concentrating research almost exclusively on magic bullets in the form of gene replacements, the medical community forecloses the less invasive option of prevention—that is, using the sophisticated new scientific understanding of the relationship between genes and environments to develop medical therapies that keep people well.

We are also concerned about the slippery slope advocates of embryo cloning have started down. If using a twelve-day-old cloned embryo for producing cells and tissues is morally acceptable, what would preclude advocates in the future from championing the harvesting of more developed cells from, say, an eight-week-old embryo, or from harvesting organs from a five-month-old cloned fetus if it were found to be a more useful medical therapy? One doesn't have to be a right-to-lifer to feel squeamish about harvesting organs from a second-trimester fetus.

Questioning Full-Birth Cloning

What about the question of cloning a full-birth human being? Today, almost no one supports full-birth cloning. Certainly, most members of Congress, on both sides of the aisle, would oppose a clonal birth. But what some supporters of therapeutic cloning don't realize is that for many in Congress, the scientific community, and the biotech industry, opposition to full-birth cloning is solely based on the fact that the cloning technique is still unsafe and could pose a risk of producing a malformed baby. Far fewer members of either party would be opposed to cloning a human baby were the procedure to become safe and reliable. After all, argue proponents, if an infertile couple desires to pass on their genetic inheritance by producing clones of one or both partners, shouldn't they be able to exercise their right of choice in the newly emerging biotech marketplace? We need not worry about the possibility of producing truly identical people, proponents argue, since, even though the clone will have the exact same genetic makeup as the original, he or she will develop differently because his or her life will unfold in a different social and environmental context than the donor's.

Therapeutic Cloning Is Not a Miracle Cure

Therapeutic cloning would seem to be the answer to virtually any disease one cares to mention. But can we reliably induce the transformation of stem cells into forming the desired types of tissue? No, we cannot. Have the relevant animal experiments been done to show it is at least theoretically feasible? No, they have not. Are human clones the only source of stem cells? No, they are not: adult tissues also contain stem cells that are mobilised for self-repair. Were it possible to create new tissues, do the techniques exist by which they can be induced into taking over the function of damaged tissue? No, they do not. Is it vaguely conceivable that cloning could produce replacement organs for transplantation? No.

And so history is all set to repeat itself as the public, yet again "blinded by science," is misled into believing that human cloning is a viable practical technique to "minimise human suffering."

James Le Fanu, *Human Life Review*, Winter 2001.

In all the technical and economic talk what both liberals and market libertarians miss is that the cloning of a human raises fundamental questions that go to the very nature of what it means to be a human being. From time immemorial we have thought of the birth of our progeny as a gift bestowed by God and/or a beneficent nature. We celebrate our generativity and revel in being participants in an act of creation. The coming together of sperm and egg represents a moment of utter surrender to forces outside of our control, We give part of ourselves up to another and the fusing of our maleness and femaleness results in a unique and finite new creation.

The Commodification of Life

The reason most people have an almost instinctual revulsion to cloning is that deep down, they sense that it signals the beginning of a new journey where the "gift of life" is steadily marginalized and eventually abandoned all together. In its place, the new progeny becomes the ultimate shopping experience—designed in advance, produced to specification, and purchased in the biological marketplace.

Cloning is, first and foremost, an act of "production," not creation. Using the new biotechnologies, a living being is produced with the same degree of engineering as we have come to expect on an assembly line. When we think of engineering standards, what immediately comes to mind is quality controls and predictable outcomes. That's exactly what cloning a human being is all about. For the first time in the history of our species, we can dictate, in advance, the final genetic constitution of the offspring. The child is no longer a unique creation—one of a kind—but rather an engineered reproduction.

Human cloning opens the door wide to the dawn of a commercial Brave New World. Already life science companies have leaped ahead of the political game being played out in Congress and the media by patenting both human embryos and stem cells, giving them upfront ownership and control of a new form of reproductive commerce. Many in the Left worry that the advent of human cloning, embryonic stem cell research, and, soon, designer babies, lays the groundwork for a new form of bio-colonialism in which global life science companies become the ultimate arbiters over the evolutionary process itself.

Moving Toward Commercial Eugenics

We have good reason to be concerned. While heads of state and parliamentarians wrestle with the escalating struggle between right to life advocates and researchers, a far more menacing tale is unfolding behind the scenes with enormous potential consequences for society. U.S and British scientists and biotech companies are using embryo and stem cell technology to develop the framework for a commercial eugenics civilization with profound long-term implications for the human race.

"Eugenics" is a term coined by Sir Francis Galton, the British philosopher, in the nineteenth century. It means to use breeding to both eliminate undesirable genetic traits and add desirable traits to improve the characteristics of an organism or species. When we think of eugenics, we think of

Adolf Hitler's ghoulish plan to create the "master" race. Today, however, a new commercial eugenics movement is being meticulously prepared in corporate boardrooms, far away from public scrutiny, and far different in nature from the kind of social eugenics hysteria that engulfed the world in the first half of the twentieth century.

Our story begins with a small biotech company, Roslin Bio-Med. The company was created in April 1998 by the Roslin Institute, a government-funded research institution outside Edinburgh, Scotland, where Dolly the sheep was cloned. The company was given an exclusive license to all the Roslin Institute's cloning technology for biomedical research. A year later, Roslin Bio-Med was sold to Geron, a U.S. firm headquartered in Menlo Park, California. Then, in January 2000, the British Patent Office granted a patent to Dr. Ian Wilmut for his cloning technology. The patent—now owned by Geron—covers the cloning process and all the animals produced by the cloning process. What the public doesn't know—because it has received so little attention—is that the British Patent Office granted Wilmut and his company a patent on all cloned human embryos up to the blastocyst stage of development—that's the stage where pluripotent stem cells emerge. The British government, in effect, became the first in the world to recognize a human embryo as a form of intellectual property. The UK was also the first country to sanction the use of embryos, and even cloned embryos, for the harvesting of stem cells.

The Power of the Patent

Despite British success in creating a favorable regulatory and commercial regime for the new research, it was the American company Geron that was quick to lock up the cloning technology. Even before securing the embryo patent, Geron had been quietly financing stem cell research conducted by two U.S. researchers, Dr. James A. Thomson of the University of Wisconsin and Dr. John Gearhart of Johns Hopkins University in Baltimore, Maryland. In November of 1998 both scientists announced that they had independently isolated and identified human stem cells. The breakthrough opened the door to the era of stem cell experimentation in medicine. The researchers' academic institutions immediately applied for patents and sold the exclusive licenses to use the patents to Geron. According to the terms of the Johns Hopkins agreement, Gearhart receives a share of the royalties collected on his patent. Gearhart and Johns Hopkins also own stock in Geron, and Gearhart serves as a consultant to the company. Geron, once alone in the field, is now being challenged by a competitor. Geron's founder, Michael West, broke away from the company and now heads up Advanced Cell Technology in Massachusetts. West's new company has secured its own patents on non-human embryo cloning and is experimenting on alternative ways to create human stem cells.

By securing patents on the cloning process, as well as on cloned human embryos and stem cells, companies like Geron and Advanced Cell Technology are in a position to dictate the terms for further advances in medical research using stem cells. The mass production of cloned human embryos provides an unlimited source of stem cells. The stem cells, in turn, are the progenitors of all of the 200 or so differentiated cell types that make up the biology of human life. Researchers, institutes, and other companies from around the world will have to pay Geron and Advanced Cell Technology to access either the use of the embryos or the stem cells they produce, giving the companies unprecedented market advantage. If other researchers or companies actually succeed in making specific body cells from the stem cells, they will likely have to enter into commercial licensing agreements of various kinds with Geron and Advanced Cell Technology for the right to produce the products.

Owning Human Life

What does this portend for the future? To begin with, the granting of a patent for cloned human embryos raises a formidable political question. Can commercial institutions lay claim to a potential individual human life, in the form of intellectual property, at its early stage of development? The British Patent Office has said yes. In the nineteenth century, we fought over the question of whether human beings after birth could be held as commercial property and eventually every nation abolished slavery. Now, however, we have technology that allows companies like Geron to claim potential human beings as intellectual property, at the developmental stage, between conception and birth. The question of whether commercial enterprises will be allowed to own potential human life at the developmental stage, will likely be one of the seminal political issues of the Biotech Century.

Secondly, should companies like Geron and Advanced Cell Technology be allowed to own—in the form of intellectual property—the primary human cells that are the gateway to the entire biological composition that constitutes human life? Do we risk the dawn of a new era in human history where the creation of human life itself will increasingly fall under the control of commercial forces? Will global biotech companies own the designs, the parts, and the processes that produce a human life?

The commercial implications of embryo and stem cell research need to be examined in their entirety. Failure to do so could trap all of us into a commercial eugenics future we neither anticipated nor willingly chose.

"Not to proceed with this therapeutic [cloning] research is equivalent to turning our back on one of the greatest medical advances of our time."

The Risks Associated with Human Cloning Have Been Exaggerated

James A. Byrne and John B. Gurdon

In the following viewpoint James A. Byrne and John B. Gurdon argue that the benefits of reproductive cloning—producing a child genetically identical to an individual—and therapeutic cloning—the creation of stem cells for medical uses—outweigh the risks. The authors claim that all reproductive techniques involve risks, and parents should be the ones to determine whether the risks are worth taking. The authors also assert that cloned embryonic stem cells offer the greatest potential for helping people with degenerative diseases. Gurdon, professor of cell biology at Cambridge University, is chairman of the Wellcome Cancer Research Institute. Byrne is a member of his research team.

As you read, consider the following questions:
1. In the authors' opinion, how do in vitro fertilization procedures weaken the inefficiency argument against reproductive human cloning?
2. What might happen to other currently accepted reproductive techniques if human cloning is banned due to the risk to the child, in the author's view?

James A. Byrne and John B. Gurdon, "Commentary on Human Cloning," *Differentiation*, vol. 69, 2002, pp. 154–57. Copyright © 2002 by Blackwell Wissenschafts-Verlag. Reproduced by permission of Blackwell Publishers.

Nuclear transfer (or more specifically somatic cell nuclear transfer) is a conceptually simple procedure. The nuclear material is removed from an egg, a somatic cell nucleus is inserted into that enucleated egg via microinjection or electrofusion, and the resulting reconstituted zygote is activated. The reconstituted zygote has the potential to divide into a blastocyst, and if implanted, develop into a child genetically identical to the nuclear donor. There are two fundamentally distinct types of human cloning by somatic cell nuclear transfer: reproductive cloning and therapeutic cloning. The objective of reproductive cloning is to produce a child genetically identical to an individual. This has been suggested as a last resort when an infertile couple are unable to conceive a biologically related child via any other method. The objective of therapeutic cloning is to produce embryonic stem cells that are genetically identical to a patient. These stem cells could then be differentiated into precursor replacement cells to treat one of a variety of degenerative diseases from which the patient might suffer. Several scientific and related ethical issues surrounding both types of human cloning are addressed in this commentary. However, many of the religious and moral arguments that have been associated with human cloning, are beyond our present scope.

Reproductive Human Cloning

The first Vertebrate reproductive cloning (nuclear transfer) experiments were on Amphibia. Initial success involved using embryonic donor cell nuclei, but it was soon discovered that differentiated cell nuclei could also result in cloned offspring, proving that there was no loss of genetic material as differentiation occurred. Nuclear transfer work progressed into the use of mammals in the 1970s and 80s, and resulted in the conception of the first mammal cloned from an adult cell nucleus in 1996. The birth of the cloned sheep "Dolly" was announced in *Nature* in 1997 and sparked worldwide discussion about the possibility of cloning humans. To date, sheep, cattle, mice, goats, and pigs have all been cloned from differentiated cells. Suggesting that somatic cell nuclear transfer may eventually be successful in all mammals, including humans. However, the majority of scientific opinion is opposed to the reproductive cloning of humans in view of the developmental, morphological, and physiological problems observed in mammals that had been cloned.

The first problem observed in mammalian cloning is a consistently low efficiency of reconstituted eggs developing to parturition (birth). Typically, to get one cloned animal to parturition, approximately one hundred eggs must be enucleated and reconstituted with donor somatic cell nuclei, either by electrofusion or microinjection. Thus nuclear transfer from adult or specialized cells is usually only 1% efficient. Even the highest efficiency observed in reproductive mammalian cloning from adult donor cell nuclei does not exceed 3%. If human reproductive cloning suffers from this low efficiency, then large numbers of human eggs would be needed to generate a single child. However, other human IVF [in vitro fertilization] procedures can also require large numbers of eggs, with 10–15 eggs being removed from the ovary at each operation, and commonly several such operations are required (on average) for a successful pregnancy to result. So the inefficiency argument against reproductive human cloning becomes somewhat weakened if one accepts IVF as an acceptable procedure to conceive a human child.

The Risks of Reproductive Cloning

The second scientific argument against reproductive human cloning is the frequency of developmental abnormalities that have been observed in various mammals that have been created by somatic cell nuclear transfer. The applicability of this animal data to humans has been debated . . . at a National Academy of Sciences conference in Washington, D.C. [in 2001]. Scientists at the conference who oppose reproductive human cloning pointed out that approximately a third of the mammals cloned have developmental abnormalities, most commonly a collection of defects referred to as LOS (large offspring syndrome), where the offspring is born oversized with disproportionately large internal organs, and often also has respiratory, circulatory and other problems, and that the same abnormalities would probably occur following human somatic cell nuclear transfer. Scientists also observe that there is currently no molecular technique available that could screen the entire genome for incompletely reprogrammed genes following nuclear transfer, and that any one of the 30,000 plus human genes could be incorrectly reprogrammed following nuclear transfer. Conversely, scientists who support reproductive human cloning suggest that many of the defects observed in animal cloning are due to poor culture conditions, and that culture conditions have been improved and optimized for human embryos and cells over the 23 years of IVF and other assisted reproductive technologies. They also note that LOS appears to be correlated to incorrect imprinting of the *IGF2 R* gene and that this gene is not imprinted in humans or other primates, suggesting that these species may be safer to clone. The difference in incidence of LOS defects following human and nonhuman IVF provides empirical evidence supporting this hypothesis. Also, the Rhesus monkeys that have been cloned by nuclear transfer of embryonic nuclei have shown no developmental or physiological abnormalities. This evidence suggests that humans and other primates may be less subject to defects after cloning than artiodactyls (sheep, cows, pigs) and rodents, but the evidence is not conclusive.

The incidence of congenital developmental abnormality in cloned mice is 12%, and in cloned goats it is nearly 38%. Many have therefore concluded that the risk in artiodactyls and rodents is roughly 30%. However, this estimate is highly variable between experiments and species. If [J.K.] Killian's hypothesis is correct, the incidence of developmental abnormalities following human somatic cell nuclear transfer may be significantly less than 30%. The incidence of developmental abnormality following natural sexual reproduction is 3% and is significantly higher when the maternal age is over 40. It is clear that many potential parents accept these risks to conceive a child. If human cloning is banned as a reproductive technique solely due to the risk to the child, then we may find ourselves in the untenable position of having banned other currently accepted reproductive techniques that suffer equal or higher risks. Legislation would have to be carefully worded, especially if the intent is not to ban therapeutic human cloning, a method that uses the same somatic cell nuclear transfer technology to produce cloned embryos.

Challenging Alternatives to Therapeutic Cloning

Therapeutic cloning involves the creation of a cloned blastocyst, genetically identical to a patient who suffers from a degenerative disease. That blastocyst (basically a ball of cells) can then be cultured into an embryonic stem cell line, which excludes most of the blastocyst cells, except for the inner stem cells that become immortalized. A stem cell is defined as a cell that can proliferate indefinitely and differentiate into a wide variety of cell types. The embryonic stem cells obtained from a cloned blastocyst are undifferentiated and can then be made to differentiate into precursor cells, which can be injected back into the patient to cure or treat the symptoms of the degenerative disease. Because the cells are genetically identical to the patient, they would not elicit the immune rejection response that tissue transplants normally face. Diseases that could potentially be treated by this procedure include heart disease, diabetes, Parkinson's and most other degenerative diseases. The main opposition to this research stems from the fact that this procedure uses cloning to create a human embryo, and that this embryo is then destroyed to obtain the embryonic stem (ES) cells. This has led opponents of this research to suggest the use of various alternatives, including noncloned ES cells, adult stem cells, and *in vitro* dedifferentiated stem cells.

1. Noncloned stem cells

Noncloned ES cells are derived from normally fertilized (rather than cloned) embryos, and thus this procedure is preferable to individuals and groups opposed to any form of human cloning. The problem with embryonic stem cells derived from noncloned embryos is that they would not be genetically identical to a patient and would require strong immunosuppressive drugs with their subsequent cost, inconvenience, and side effects.

2. Adult stem cells

Adult stem cells that are found in bone marrow and some other tissues have been isolated and encouraged to proliferate. Various pro-life groups have suggested that stem cell research should be restricted to these cells only, as this does not involve the destruction of human embryos or cloning techniques. However, adult stem cells have some fundamental disadvantages when compared to embryonic stem cells. They are hard to isolate and have restricted proliferation potential; furthermore, the range of cells they can be differentiated into is limited. There is a lack of identified stem cells for most tissues. There have been reports of adult stem cells transdifferentiating, for example, from a haematopoietic (bone marrow derived) fate into a neural fate [the end result of cell development], and continued research into adult stem cells is certainly recommended, but the fact remains that by far the greatest therapeutic potential lies with embryonic stem cells.

Keefe. © 2003 by Cagle Cartoons. Reproduced by permission.

3. *In vitro* dedifferentiated stem cells

The ideal situation would be to obtain embryonic stem cells by directly dedifferentiating normal body cells *in vitro*. While not yet achieved, research into nuclear reprogramming is currently being performed precisely for this reason. This situation would have all the therapeutic benefits of undifferentiated genetically identical embryonic stem cells without the ethical problem of having to destroy a human embryo.

The alternatives to therapeutic human cloned ES cells are either unfeasible with today's technology (*in vitro* dedifferentiated stem cells) or of relatively limited therapeutic potential (adult stem cells, noncloned ES cells). Embryonic stem cells obtained by transfer of nuclei from adult cells to enucleated eggs offer the greatest therapeutic potential, with today's technology, for tissue replacement therapy.

Focusing the Scientific Debate

The scientific debate around reproductive human cloning centres on the right of an infertile individual or couple to reproduce without governmental interference, set against the right of the child not to be exposed to an excessively high risk of developmental abnormality. What is regarded as "excessive risk" for the child is clearly subjective, with different potential parents in different situations inevitably having different perceptions of what is an acceptable risk to conceive a biologically related child. If the risk of developmental abnormality and/or perinatal death following human somatic cell nuclear transfer could be proven to be lower than that 3% observed from sexual reproduction, a significant proportion of the scientific opposition would cease, but opposition would no doubt remain from religious and other ethical quarters. The prudent suggestion would be to perform extensive primate nuclear transfers before an informed scientific decision could be reached either for or against this reproductive technology. There is currently insufficient empirical evidence to convincingly establish that the technology is intrinsically safe or unsafe (from the potential offspring's perspective) in either humans or other primates.

The scientific debate regarding therapeutic human cloning revolves around the therapeutic benefits against the ethical cost of destroying the early cloned embryo. Many allocate to the early embryo the status of an individual with fundamental human rights and consider the destruction of that embryo equivalent to murder. Several details should be considered when debating the issue. The early mammalian embryo is a ball of cells without even a rudimentary nervous system, and the division of this ball of cells into two or more parts results in two or more monozygotic twins. Thus whether this early embryo can yet be classified as an "individual" is questionable. Abortion legislation in most countries has already established that the rights and choices of grown adults supersede the rights of the early embryo. Most embryos (> 70%) that result from natural sexual reproduction do not implant into the uterine endometrium. If each of these embryos has fundamental human rights, this would make premeditated attempts at pregnancy by natural sexual reproduction the logical equivalent of mass murder. The ethical considerations basically come down to our society's value system. Which is of greater value, the life of an adult or child dying from a degenerative disease, or a 5-day-old embryo that is little more than a ball of cells?

In summary, the risks associated with reproductive human cloning have not been conclusively established. Perhaps future research will establish the safety of the procedure for both mother and child, but other ethical and religious objections would almost certainly remain. With our current level of scientific and technological skills, therapeutic human cloning has the greatest medical potential in comparison to its suggested alternatives. Not to proceed with this therapeutic research is equivalent to turning our backs on one of the greatest medical advances of our time and condemning millions of adults and children to a premature death or a life of intense misery and suffering. Is this the brave new world we wish to live in?

"If anyone should be wary of medical techniques to 'improve' ordinary reproduction—as [genetic engineering] purports to do—it's women."

Genetic Engineering Threatens Women's Reproductive Choices

Judith Levine

History has shown that "improvements" in reproductive technology can harm women, and technologies that use genetic engineering to help women become pregnant and select their child's genetic makeup are no exception, argues Judith Levine in the following viewpoint. The industry that promotes these new reproductive technologies is more interested in profit than promoting women's reproductive health, she maintains. According to Levine, prenatal genetic modification—the alteration of an embryo's genes—does not increase reproductive choice for all women, just those who can afford it. Moreover, claims Levine, women cannot give informed consent when agreeing to genetic engineering fertility procedures when the risks are unknown. Levine, who writes on women's issues for magazines such as *Ms.*, *Oxygen*, and *Salon*, is author of *My Enemy, My Love: Women, Men, and the Dilemma of Gender.*

As you read, consider the following questions:

1. According to the author, what will happen when scientists perfect inheritable genetic alterations on mice?
2. In Levine's opinion, what must prevail over individual choice when it comes to species-altering procedures?

Judith Levine, "What Human Genetic Modification Means for Women," *WorldWatch*, vol. 15, July/August 2002, pp. 26–29. Copyright © 2002 by World Watch Institute. All rights reserved. Reproduced by permission.

S educed by the medical promises of genetic science or
fearful of losing reproductive autonomy, many feminists
have been slow to oppose human genetic engineering. But
GE is a threat to women, and in the broadest sense a feminist issue. Here's why.

If anyone should be wary of medical techniques to "improve" ordinary reproduction—as GE purports to do—it's
women. History is full of such "progress," and its grave results. When limbless babies were born to mothers who took
thalidomide, the drug was recalled. But the deadly results of
another "pregnancy-enhancing" drug, DES, showed up only
years later, as cancer in the daughters of DES mothers. The
high-estrogen Pill was tested first on uninformed Puerto Ri-
can mothers, some of whom may have died from it.

Today's fertility industry takes in $4 billion a year, even
though in-vitro fertilization (IVF) succeeds in only 3 of 10
cases. Virtually unregulated and highly competitive, these
fertility doctors often undertake experimental treatments.
Recently, the Institute for Reproductive Medicine and Science at New Jersey's St. Barnabas Medical Center announced
the success of a new fertility "therapy" called cytoplasmic
transfer, in which some of the cellular material outside the
nucleus of one woman's egg is transferred into the egg of another woman who is having difficulty sustaining embryo survival. The transferred cytoplasm contains mitochondria (or-
ganelles that produce energy for the cell), which have a small
number of their own genes. So the embryo produced with cytoplasmic transfer can end up with two genetic mothers. This
mixing, called "mitochondrial heteroplasmy," can cause life-
threatening symptoms that don't show up until later in life.
When the Public Broadcasting Service's *Nova* enthusiastically
reported on the procedure, complete with footage of its cute
outcome, Katy, it mentioned no risks.

Didn't these patients give informed consent? Yes and no.
Most read warnings and signed their names. But with genetic therapies there's no such thing as "informed," says Judy
Norsigian of the Boston Women's Health Collective, "because the risks can't be known." Adds biologist Ruth Hubbard, the deadliness of DES was discovered "only because it
showed itself in an otherwise very rare condition. If the ef-

fects [of human genetic engineering] are delayed, and if they are not associated with a particularly unusual pathology, it could take quite a long time to find out." Or indeed, "we might never know."

Experimenting on Women and Children

Scottish biologist Ian Wilmut, the "father" of the famously first-cloned sheep Dolly, provided these statistics in 2001: Of the 31,007 sheep, mice, pig, and other mammal eggs that had undergone somatic cell nuclear transfer (cloning), 9,391 viable embryos resulted. From those embryos came 267 live-born offspring. In these animals, *The New York Times* reported, "random errors" were ubiquitous—including fatal heart and lung defects, malfunctioning immune systems, and grotesque obesity. In all, "fewer than 3 percent of all cloning efforts succeed." Dolly may be a victim of accelerated aging, another problem in cloned animals. In January [2002], it was reported that she has arthritis, at the unusually early age of five and a half. Mothers of clones are endangered too, since their bodies have trouble supporting the abnormally large fetuses that cloning often produces.

It's likely that scientists will get better at cloning animals, and at the more complex procedures required to produce inheritable genetic alterations. Then, as health activists quip, if it works on a mouse, they will try it on a woman. The problem, warns Stuart Newman, a cell biologist at New York Medical College in Valhalla, is that if it works on a mouse, it is likely *not* to work on a woman: "Every species presents a new set of problems." How might the process be perfected in human? In clinical trials?

"The degree of risk to be taken should never exceed that determined by the humanitarian importance of the problem to be solved by the experiment," reads the Nuremburg Code, drawn up after World War II to forbid future torturous experiments of the sort Nazi "scientists" inflicted on concentration-camp inmates. What is the humanitarian importance of creating a faster 100-meter sprinter? Or even curing a disease with genetic engineering when other options are still untried? The science to find "safe" means of human GE, says Newman, would constitute "an entirely experimental enterprise with little justification." In other words, "We can't get there from here."

We Are Not Our Genes

When the Human Genome Project finished its map of our DNA, its press releases called it the "blueprint" of humanity, the very Book of Life. The newspapers had already been filling up with reports of the discovery of a "gene for" breast cancer, and a "gene for" gayness. Many people had begun to believe our genes determine who we become.

This line of thinking should sound familiar to women. Not long ago, we were told that hormones, not sexism, explained why there has never been a U.S. female president (she might start a nuclear war in a fit of PMS [premenstrual syndrome]). A decade after that came the notion that gender is "hard-wired" into the brain. Not incidentally, these claims were made just when social movements were proving Simone de Beauvoir's adage that women are not born but made. Now the old determinism is raising its ugly head once again, with genetics. As "non-traditional" families finally bring legitimacy to social parenting, proponents of inheritable genetic modification tell us not only that we can predetermine the natures of our children, but that cloning is the only means by which gays and lesbians can become real parents. "Real" parental ties, they imply, are biological, genetic.

"Genetic determinism" is not biologically accurate. "It is very unlikely that a simple and directly causal link between genes and most common diseases will ever be found," writes Richard Horton, editor of the British medical journal *The Lancet*. If this is true of disease, it is even more true of musicality, optimism, or sexual orientation. The more complex a trait, the less useful genetics are to explain it. Hubbard writes, "The lens of genetics really is one of the narrowest foci to define our biology, not to mention what our social being is about."

Genetic Modification Is Not a Reproductive Choice

For feminists, one of the most galling aspects of the debate about human genetic manipulation is the way its proponents have hijacked the language or "choice" to sell its products. IVF clinics and biotech research shouldn't be regulated, say the companies that run them, because that would impinge on "choice" (for the paying customers, if not for their unsuspecting offspring). The Book of Life is becoming a "catalogue" of "consumer eugenics," says sociologist Barbara Katz Rothman.

Some ethicists, too, have posited a reproductive "right" to

The Impact of Research Cloning on Women

- Research cloning is a highly inefficient process, which would require an unlimited supply of human eggs. It has been estimated that research cloning might be able to provide up to 1.7 million therapies per year. Assuming a highly optimistic success rate of 1 stem cell culture per 5 cloned embryos, and 1 cloned embryo per 10 eggs, these therapies would require 85 million eggs, or 8.5 million egg donors.

- Egg donation is a burdensome, risky, and painful procedure. Egg donation is not a simple process; it lasts several weeks, and includes repeated injections of fertility hormones and super-ovulatory drugs and finally, surgery. Risks associated with egg extraction include a potential link to ovarian cysts and cancers, severe pelvic pain, abdominal bleeding, and ovarian hyperstimulation syndrome, a potentially life-threatening condition.

- An explosion in demand for human eggs would exacerbate the coercive nature of the lucrative egg donation industry. Currently, compensation to women for egg "donation" is uncapped, and ranges from an average payment of $5,000–6,000 to as high as $80,000. The increase in egg demand created by research cloning is likely to increase the price of eggs and coercive potential of the egg market.

- The burden of egg supply will likely fall on underprivileged women. There are no federal standards concerning limitations on the number of times a woman can donate eggs. Low-income women may feel obliged to choose repeated egg donation as a source of income.

- Research cloning will result in a loss of choice for women. Researchers can clone embryos from any number of body cells. A woman's cells could be removed for the creation of any number of cloned embryos without her knowledge or choice.

Andrew Kimbrell, testimony before the U.S. Senate Committee on Commerce, Science and Transportation, March 27, 2003.

---

prenatal baby design. People decide whether or not to reproduce based on an expected "package of experiences," wrote John Robertson, an influential bioethicist, in 1998. "Since the makeup of the packet will determine whether or not they reproduce . . . some right to choose characteristics, either by negative exclusion or positive selection, should follow as well." Already, selective abortion is widely accepted after prenatal genetic screening uncovers an "anomaly." Although some (notably disability rights activists) critique such "negative eugenics," many people accept this practice for serious medical conditions. In any case, selecting from among a small number of embryos is a far cry from rearranging the DNA of a future child to achieve some preferred traits.

What feminists mean by "choice"—the ability to control fertility with safe and legal birth control and abortion—is far more concrete. It confers existential equality on the female half of the human race, which is why women worldwide have sought it for centuries. But genetic engineering designs in inequality: it will artificially confer heritable advantages only on those who can afford to buy them. Performed prenatally, moreover, it affects the new person without that person's prior consent and possibly to her physical or emotional detriment. "Ending an unwanted pregnancy is apples, and mucking around with genes is oranges," says Marcy Darnovsky of the Center for Genetics and Society. "We support abortion rights because we support a right to not have a child—or to have one. But we don't support a woman's right to do anything to that child once it's alive, like abuse it or kill it." Ironically, as Lisa Handwerker of the National Women's Health Network has pointed out, anti-choice, anti-GE forces share with GE's proponents an obsessive focus on the embryo as an independent entity, while they both virtually ignore the pregnant woman and the child she may bear.

Bans Do Not Give Fetuses Rights

Some choice advocates fear that any perceived concern *about* embryos will cede territory to anti-abortionists, who want full legal protection *of* embryos and fetuses. U.S. Congressman Henry Waxman reflected this confusion when he said at a Congressional hearing, "I do not believe that the Congress should prohibit potentially life-saving research on genetic cell replication because it accords a cell—a special cell, but only a cell—the same rights and protections as a person."

But pro-choice opponents of cloning do not propose to give cells rights. Rather, we worry that cloned embryos might be implanted by unscrupulous fertility entrepreneurs into desperate women, where they'll grow into cloned humans. And from cloning, it is not a big step to designing children.

For legal, political, and philosophical reasons, University of Chicago medical ethicist Mary Mahowald proposes clarifying the pro-choice position. "It does feminist support for abortion no good to confuse life with personhood," she told me. "We can admit that the embryo is life and therefore afford it respect—the respect, for instance, of not exchanging it genes with those of another cell. But respecting life is not the same as granting rights. Rights are reserved for living persons."

"We're against bans," said a member of a coalition of mainstream reproductive-rights groups, explaining why the coalition was reluctant to join a campaign against human cloning. This reaction is not surprising in the United States, where defense of personal freedom can often trump the public interest.

Women's liberation means more than personal freedom, though. Rooted in the Left, feminism is a critique of all kinds of domination and therefore a vision of an egalitarian world—racially and economically, as well as sexually.

In the case of species-altering procedures, social justice must prevail over individual "choice." Arguing for an international ban on reproductive cloning and regulation of related research, Patricia Baird, chair of Canada's Royal Commission on New Reproductive Technologies, put it this way: "The framework of individual autonomy and reproductive choice is dangerously incomplete, because it leaves out the effects on others and on social systems, and the effects on the child and future generations." The good news is that good public policy protects individuals too. Baird offered the example of overfishing, which might benefit the fisherman in the short run but deplete the fishery for everyone, including that fisherman, in the long run. Regulation sustains his and his children's livelihoods. "We all have a stake in the kind of community we live in," Baird said.

"Through the extension and development of reproductive technologies, women will have more control over their bodies."

Genetic Engineering Protects Women's Reproductive Choices

George Dvorsky

In the following viewpoint George Dvorsky argues that genetic engineering gives women more reproductive control. In fact, he claims, women can prevent disease in their offspring through genetic modification before their children are born, which is more proactive than terminating a pregnancy when an embryo shows signs of disease. Moreover, Dvorsky asserts, women have always used the latest available technology, such as prenatal screening and vaccines, to enhance their children's chances of living healthy, successful lives, and genetic modification simply gives women more options. Dvorsky is a staff writer for betterhumans.com, a website that explores and advocates the use of science and technology for furthering human progress.

As you read, consider the following questions:

1. In Dvorsky's opinion, why is there little interest in feminist bioethics?
2. What should women be more concerned about than the "perfect-baby fallacy," in the author's view?
3. According to Dvorsky, how might a ban on inheritable genetic modification hurt women?

It's hard to decide which is more frustrating, the proposal or the lack of uproar from women's groups.

On November 1, 2002, the World Congress of Bioethics will conduct a special session in Brazil entitled "Towards an International Ethical, Social and Political Accord on Human Cloning and Human Species-Alteration."

A memorandum sent out to conference attendees in advance of the session explicitly targets women's groups. "Supporters of women's health and reproductive rights have particularly pressing reasons for concern over human cloning and inheritable genetic modification (IGM).[1] Human cloning and IGM could not be developed without unethical experimentation on women and children," it notes.

"These technologies would diminish women's control over their reproductive decisions, and subject them to pressures to produce the 'perfect baby,'" it goes on. "Some advocates of cloning and IGM are attempting to appropriate the language of reproductive choice, blurring the critical difference between the right to terminate an unwanted pregnancy and the selection of a future child's genetic makeup."

After reading the memorandum, I was flabbergasted. Are the authors—Richard Hayes, executive director of the Center for Genetics and Society, and Rosario Isasi, of the University of Toronto—actually suggesting that strict limitations and moratoriums on inheritable genetic modification will help women retain the rights necessary for reproductive choice and autonomy?

Few Feminists Fight

As far as I'm concerned, this is another affront to women's entitlements to control their body's reproductive processes.

---

1. Human cloning involves the replacement of the DNA in a female egg with the DNA of another person. When this egg is implanted into the womb of the mother, as in in vitro fertilization, the embryo develops into a fetus and is born after nine months, just like any other baby. The cloned baby shares the same exact DNA as the person whose DNA was injected into the egg cell, not unlike identical twins. A couple that is unable to conceive and does not want to use the DNA of another person might choose to use the DNA of one parent; thus producing an identical twin of that parent. No case of human cloning has yet been officially documented. IGM alters the genes in early embryos. Parents who choose IGM may hope to prevent their child from inheriting a debilitating or deadly disease or perhaps even determine their child's physical attributes such as hair or eye color.

So why have so few women spoken out?

After seeing little feminist reaction to the Hayes and Isasi memorandum, I'm forced to acknowledge a dangerous vacuum in Transhumanist [one who believes human beings can be improved by science and technology] and progressive bioethicist circles: there are very few vocal feminists fighting for women's rights to control the genetic makeup of their offspring.

The most well-known Transhumanist feminist I can think of is Donna Haraway, who in 1984 famously wrote "A Manifesto for Cyborgs: Science, Technology, and Socialist Feminism in the 1980s." In the manifesto, Haraway proposed that women use technology to further liberate themselves from limited and constraining biological processes. But only a few people jumped on board—such as Gill Kirkup, Linda Janes, Kathryn Woodward, Fiona Hovenden and Anne Balsamo.

Why such little interest in feminist bioethics? After thinking about the problem, I propose three possible reasons:

1. *Techno-culture:* Transhumanism and other future-oriented movements tend to be dominated by educated white males that have been immersed in computer and related technology cultures. The dearth of women pursuing science and technology careers has contributed to this situation.

2. *Naturalistic focus:* Contemporary feminism has been quite hostile and suspicious of futurists in general, preferring to celebrate naturalistic womanhood and female biological processes.

3. *Inadequate outreach:* Perhaps most significantly, progressive bioethicists have done an inadequate job of reaching out to the feminist community. In many ways it is our fault—and not the fault of the feminists—that the use of future reproductive technologies has not become a feminist issue.

So, what should feminist bioethicists be concerned about? A quick run-through of the World Congress of Bioethics letter reveals several important issues and misconceptions that should be immediately addressed.

The Perfect-Baby Fallacy

The first is the perfect-baby fallacy. With human cloning and inheritable genetic modification, Hayes and Isasi are concerned that women will be compelled to have "perfect babies." In their mind, this would decrease women's reproductive control and choice. In my mind, women should be more concerned about pressure from governments and misinformed special-interest groups that force them to reject progressive and beneficial health technologies. Through the extension and development of reproductive technologies, women will have more control over their bodies, not less.

Human Cloning Is Just Another Form of Reproduction

If the freedom to reproduce is a basic human right—wanting to have and raise a biological child is a powerful, if seemingly irrational, force that people experiencing it have trouble explaining—then no free society should ban reproductive cloning.

When perfected, cloning will produce nothing less and nothing more than an unpredictable son or daughter to love and to hold. Baby-making is to be judged not on the technique or technology involved but the love a parent gives the child, natural or clonal, after it is born.

Andy Ho, *Straits Times*, April 12, 2003.

Not only that, trying to achieve "perfect babies" is something women have always done, adapting new methods and technologies as they become available. Before and during pregnancies today, for example, women take folic acid to reduce the chance that their baby will be born with spina bifida. In addition, most women have prenatal screening, stop drinking and smoking, strive to eat a healthier and more balanced diet, take prenatal exercise classes, rest their bodies as much as possible and often take early maternity leave.

And even after babies are born, most women don't stop wanting the best for them. They will read about the latest in parenting—in everything from psychology books to parenting magazines. They will also make efforts to socialize children as responsibly as possible, aiming to place their kids in the best available daycares and schools. And they will most likely have their kids vaccinated, see a doctor regularly for a checkup and see a specialist for any cognitive or physical problems.

Once more technologies are available to ensure healthy children, women using them will not be bowing down to social pressures to create "perfect babies." Rather, they will do what they have always done: they will endeavor to have the healthiest and fittest children as is medically possible.

Finding Little Difference Between Termination and Selection

The second thing feminist bioethicists should be concerned about is the distinction between termination and choice. Hayes and Isasi claim that there is a critical difference between the right to terminate an unwanted pregnancy and the selection of a future child's genetic makeup. I am having great trouble trying to understand what this "critical" difference is.

Currently, couples have very little control over the makeup of their offspring. A child's genetic characteristics are fixed at the point of conception, and prospective parents pray that he or she will be strong and healthy and won't have genetic diseases.

If an embryo does show signs of disease, women can terminate a pregnancy. It seems only logical then that we should extend this right to the prevention of diseases in the first place—giving couples the control they have always sought but that to date has only been available in a crude form.

So despite what Hayes and Isasi claim, there is very little difference between termination and selection. They are on the same spectrum, and in some ways selection is merely a more proactive approach.

The Risks of an Outright Ban

Now, all this isn't to say that I'm in favour of rampant cloning and genetic modification. As Hayes and Isasi rightfully point out, human cloning and inheritable genetic modification could lead to unethical experimentation on women and children. Also, both are grossly underdeveloped and even dangerous today.

But this is no reason to ban them outright. It is a reason for proper monitoring and development. An outright ban would only drive cloning and genetic modification underground, where it may hurt women in the same way as clandestine abortions.

Unless feminists get involved, however, a ban may very well be what we get, as conservative bioethicists use the veil of women's rights to implement their agenda. The lack of vocal opposition gives the impression of agreement and support. Is this really in women's best interest?

| "*Cloning endangered species . . . has an important place in plans to manage species that are in danger of extinction.*"

Cloning Could Save Endangered Species

Robert P. Lanza, Betsy L. Dresser, and Philip Damiani

Robert P. Lanza, Betsy L. Dresser, and Philip Damiani claim in the following viewpoint that cloning provides a new way to preserve endangered species. According to the authors, cloning could even in some cases resurrect recently extinct species. Although preserving endangered species' habitat is important, some countries are too poor or unstable to do so; thus storing the genetic stock of threatened animals from these countries may be the only way to preserve at-risk species, the authors argue. Lanza is vice president of Advanced Cell Technology (ACT); Dresser is director of the Audubon Institute Center for Research of Endangered Species; Damiani, a research scientist at ACT, is a member of the International Embryo Transfer Society.

As you read, consider the following questions:
1. According to the authors, why must researchers get cells from two different species to yield the clone of one?
2. What do the efficiency statistics of cloning reflect, in the authors' view?
3. In the authors' opinion, what difficulties are faced by researchers who are trying to clone already extinct species?

In late November [2000] a humble Iowa cow is slated to give birth to the world's first cloned endangered species, a baby bull to be named Noah. Noah is a gaur: a member of a species of large oxlike animals that are now rare in their homelands of India, Indochina and southeast Asia. These one-ton bovines have been hunted for sport for generations. More recently the gaur's habitats of forests, bamboo jungles and grasslands have dwindled to the point that only roughly 36,000 are thought to remain in the wild. The World Conservation Union–IUCN Red Data Book lists the gaur as endangered, and trade in live gaur or gaur products—whether horns, hides or hooves—is banned by the Convention on International Trade in Endangered Species (CITES).

But if all goes as predicted, in a few weeks a spindly-legged little Noah will trot in a new day in the conservation of his kind as well as in the preservation of many other endangered species. Perhaps most important, he will be living, mooing proof that one animal can carry and give birth to the exact genetic duplicate, or clone, of an animal of a different species. And Noah will be just the first creature up the ramp of the ark of endangered species that we and other scientists are currently attempting to clone: plans are under way to clone the African bongo antelope, the Sumatran tiger and that favorite of zoo lovers, the reluctant-to-reproduce giant panda. Cloning could also reincarnate some species that are already extinct—most immediately, perhaps, the bucardo mountain goat of Spain. The last bucardo—a female—died of a smashed skull when a tree fell on it but . . . Spanish scientists have preserved some of its cells.

Introducing New Genes into the Pool

Advances in cloning offer a way to preserve and propagate endangered species that reproduce poorly in zoos until their habitats can be restored and they can be reintroduced to the wild. Cloning's main power, however, is that it allows researchers to introduce new genes back into the gene pool of a species that has few remaining animals. Most zoos are not equipped to collect and cryopreserve semen; similarly, eggs are difficult to obtain and are damaged by freezing. But by cloning animals whose body cells have been preserved, scientists can keep the genes of that individual alive, maintaining (and in some instances increasing) the overall genetic diversity of endangered populations of that species.

Nevertheless, some conservation biologists have been slow to recognize the benefits of basic assisted reproduction strategies, such as in vitro fertilization, and have been hesitant to consider cloning. Although we agree that every effort should be made to preserve wild spaces for the incredible diversity of life that inhabits this planet, in some cases either the battle has already been lost or its outcome looks dire. Cloning technology is not a panacea, but it offers the opportunity to save some of the species that contribute to that diversity. A clone still requires a mother, however, and very few conservationists would advocate rounding up wild female endangered animals for that purpose or subjecting a precious zoo resident of the same species to the rigors of assisted reproduction and surrogate motherhood. That means that to clone an endangered species, researchers such as ourselves must solve the problem of how to get cells from two different species to yield the clone of one.

A Gaur Is Born

It is a deceptively simple-looking process. A needle jabs through the protective layer, or zona pellucida, surrounding an egg that hours ago resided in a living ovary. In one deft movement, a research assistant uses it to suck out the egg's nucleus—which contains the majority of a cell's genetic material—leaving behind only a sac of gel called cytoplasm. Next he uses a second needle to inject another, whole cell under the egg's outer layer. With the flip of an electric switch, the cloning is complete: the electrical pulse fuses the introduced cell to the egg, and the early embryo begins to divide. In a few days, it will become a mass of cells large enough to implant into the uterus of a surrogate-mother animal previously treated with hormones. In a matter of months, that surrogate mother will give birth to a clone.

In practice, though, this technique—which scientists call nuclear transfer—is not so easy. To create Noah, we at Advanced Cell Technology (ACT) in Worcester, Mass., had to fuse skin cells taken from a male gaur with 692 enucleated cow eggs. As we report in [a 2000] issue of the journal *Cloning*, of those 692 cloned early embryos, only 81 grew in the laboratory into blastocysts, balls of 100 or so cells that are sufficiently developed to implant for gestation. We ended up inserting 42 blastocysts into 32 cows, but only eight became pregnant. We removed the fetuses from two of the pregnant cows for scientific analysis; four other animals experienced spontaneous abortions in the second or third month of the usual nine-month pregnancy; and the seventh cow had a very unexpected late-term spontaneous abortion in August [2000].

The statistics of the efficiency of cloning reflect the fact that the technology is still as much an art as it is a science—particularly when it involves transplanting an embryo into another species. Scientists, including those of us at ACT, have had the highest success rates cloning domestic cattle implanted into cows of the same species. But even in this instance we have had to work hard to produce just a few animals. For every 100 cow eggs we fuse with adult cattle cells, we can expect only between 15 and 20 to produce blastocysts. And only roughly 10 percent of those—one or two—yield live births.

The numbers reflect difficulties with the nuclear transfer process itself, which we are now working to understand. They are also a function of the vagaries of assisted reproduction technology.

Determining the Species to Be Cloned

Accordingly, we expect that the first few endangered species to be cloned will be those whose reproduction has already been well studied. Several zoos and conservation societies—including the Audubon Institute Center for Research of Endangered Species (AICRES) in New Orleans . . .—have probed the reproductive biology of a range of endangered species, with some notable successes. [In November 1999], for example, [Betsy L.] Dresser and her colleagues reported the first transplantation of a previously frozen embryo of an endangered animal into another species that resulted in a live birth. In this case, an ordinary house cat gave birth to an African wildcat, a species that has declined in some areas.

So far, beyond the African wildcat and the gaur, we and others have accomplished interspecies embryo transfers in four additional cases: an Indian desert cat into a domestic cat; a bongo antelope into a more common African antelope called an eland; a mouflon sheep into a domestic sheep; and a rare red deer into a common white-tailed deer. All yielded live births. We hope that the studies of felines will pave the way for cloning the cheetah, of which only roughly 12,000 remain in southern Africa. The prolonged courtship behavior of cheetahs requires substantial territory, a possible explanation for why the animals have bred so poorly in zoos and yet another reason to fear their extinction as their habitat shrinks. . . .

Saving the Bongo

AICRES scientists hope to take advantage of the success with bongo antelope that one of us (Dresser) had while at the Cincinnati Zoo. In 1984 Dresser and Charles Earle Pope of the University of Alabama at Birmingham (now with AICRES and Louisiana State University) and their colleagues announced the birth of a bongo after moving very early embryos from a pregnant female bongo to an eland surrogate mother.

Most of the mountain subspecies of bongo—a medium-size antelope with vertical white stripes—live in captivity. According to the World Conservation Union–IUCN, the mountain bongo is endangered, with only 50 or so remaining in a small region of Kenya. In contrast, the 1999 Bongo International Studbook lists nearly 550 mountain bongo living in zoos throughout the world. The lowland bongo subspecies is slightly better off: it is listed as "near threatened" and has a population of perhaps several thousand scattered throughout central and western Africa.

A coalition of conservation organizations in the U.S. and Kenya is now planning to send mountain bongo that have been bred in captivity to two sites in Kenya. And in a new approach to reintroducing a species, AICRES is working in Kenya to transfer frozen bongo embryos into eland surrogates. Cloning could support these efforts and possibly yield more bongo for reintroduction.

Cloning Extinct Animals

But what about animals that are already extinct? Chances are slim to nil that scientists will soon be able to clone dinosaurs, à la *Jurassic Park*, or woolly mammoths. The primary problem is the dearth of preserved tissue—and hence DNA. A group of researchers unearthed what they had hoped would be a well-preserved mammoth [in 1999], but repeated freezing and thawing over the eons had poked holes in the creature's DNA, and molecular biologists have not yet found a feasible way of filling in such genetic gaps.

A similar difficulty has hobbled efforts by Australian scientists to clone a thylacine, or Tasmanian tiger, a wolflike marsupial that died out in the 1930s. Researchers at the Australian Museum in Sydney are attempting to clone cells from a thylacine pup that was preserved in alcohol in 1866, but the DNA is in such poor condition that they say they will have to reconstruct all of the animal's chromosomes.

A New Preservation Tool

Cloning techniques may become instrumental in rescuing endangered species—and possibly reversing extinctions that have already occurred. Conservations have used captive propagation programs to preserve endangered species in captivity. Limitations such as restricted physical space for animals, problems with animal husbandry, and general reproductive failure of the animals have created the need for additional propagation programs. Most ethicists who strongly oppose human cloning see no problem in using the technique to rescue endangered species.

Applied Genetic News, October 2000.

The recently extinct bucardo may prove a more promising target for resurrection. ACT is arranging a collaboration with Alberto Fernández-Arias and José Folch of the Agricultural Research Service in Zaragoza, Spain. Fernández-Arias froze tissue from the last bucardo. He and Folch had tried for several years to preserve the mountain goat, which in the end was wiped out by poaching, habitat destruction and landslides. [In 1999] they transferred embryos from a subspecies related to the bucardo to a domestic goat, yielding live kids.

But even if interspecies nuclear transfer succeeds for the

bucardo, it will yield only a sorority of clones, because we have tissue from just one animal, a female. ACT plans to try to make a male by removing one copy of the X chromosome from one of the female bucardo's cells and using a tiny artificial cell called a microsome to add a Y chromosome from a closely related goat species. The technology has been used by other researchers to manipulate human chromosomes, but it has never before been used for cloning. A nonprofit organization called the Soma Foundation has been established to help fund such efforts.

Why Clone?

Cloning endangered species is controversial, but we assert that it has an important place in plans to manage species that are in danger of extinction. Some researchers have argued against it, maintaining that it would restrict an already dwindling amount of genetic diversity for those species. Not so. We advocate the establishment of a worldwide network of repositories to hold frozen tissue from all the individuals of an endangered species from which it is possible to collect samples. Those cells—like the sperm and eggs now being collected in "frozen zoos" by a variety of zoological parks—could serve as a genetic trust for reconstituting entire populations of a given species. Such an enterprise would be relatively inexpensive: a typical three-foot freezer can hold more than 2,000 samples and uses just a few dollars of electricity per year. Currently only AICRES and the San Diego Zoo's Center for Reproduction of Endangered Species maintain banks of frozen body cells that could be used for cloning.

Other critics claim that the practice could overshadow efforts to preserve habitat. We counter that while habitat preservation is the keystone of species conservation, some countries are too poor or too unstable to support sustainable conservation efforts. What is more, the continued growth of the human species will probably make it impossible to save enough habitat for some other species. Cloning by interspecies nuclear transfer offers the possibility of keeping the genetic stock of those species on hand without maintaining populations in captivity, which is a particularly costly enterprise in the case of large animals.

Another argument against cloning endangered species is that it might siphon donor money away from habitat maintenance. But not all potential donors are willing to support efforts to stem the tide of habitat destruction. We should recognize that some who would otherwise not donate to preserve endangered species at all might want to support cloning or other assisted reproduction technologies.

The time to act is now.

"What does it mean to save a species if and when its habitat is being destroyed?"

Cloning May Not Be Enough to Save Endangered Species

Ellen Goodman

Scientists are using advanced biotechnology to clone endangered species while at the same time people are destroying the animals' habitats, claims Ellen Goodman in the following viewpoint. Using biotechnology to save endangered species is admirable, Goodman grants, but she questions the point of cloning threatened animals when their native habitats are disappearing. Goodman argues that those concerned about endangered species should look beyond the individual animal and focus on preserving habitats and animal communities. Goodman, a syndicated columnist, is associate editor at the *Boston Globe*.

As you read, consider the following questions:

1. In Goodman's opinion, what other biotech procedures besides cloning have been used to save endangered species?
2. What does Goodman claim is the stunning gap in the environmental behavior of our own species?
3. According to Goodman, what larger ark should people be thinking about?

In Iowa there is a cow as ordinary as her name: Bessie. Only one thing distinguishes Bessie from the rest of the herd: she is about to give birth to a gaur instead of a calf.

No one knows what this Midwestern mother will make of her foreign offspring.

Will she regard the ox-like Asian animal as an ugly duckling of a cow? Or a swan of a son?

This is not a character out of a Hans Christian Andersen fairy tale.

It's science, not fiction—a story of endangered species and reproductive technology, of human creation and, I suppose, human destruction.

Our gal Bessie is the surrogate mother of the world's first cloned endangered species.

The animal she is carrying was cloned from a single cell of a dead gaur and implanted by scientists from Advanced Cell Technology for a cross-species pregnancy.

A Biotech Ark

These researchers have given the bull-to-be a name of biblical proportions. They call him "Noah."

He is, after all, born to be the first passenger on an ark they are building as a rescue ship from environmental catastrophe.

The "spindly-legged little Noah will trot in a new day in the conservation of his kind as well as in the preservation of many other endangered species," write the scientists who cloned and implanted this offspring.

In *Scientific American*, they say he will "be just the first creature up the ramp of the ark of endangered species."

Well, I want to share their birthday celebration. This is, after all, progress in the biotech ability to save a species, one member at a time.

We have already seen in-vitro fertilization of both a panda and a gorilla. We've had a cross-species pregnancy between antelopes. And [in 1999] an ordinary house cat gave birth to an African wild cat.

Now, those who put Noah in Bessie's womb plan to clone an endangered Sumatran tiger, and even an extinct bucardo mountain goat.

No Replacement for Protecting Habitat

Being able to clone animals may mean that the habitats of these animals are less protected. The destruction of habitat is one of the leading causes for population decline. Being able to clone animals would mean that animals that often will not reproduce in captivity could be cloned instead. Cloning may seem like an easy way out instead of protecting the natural habitat of these animals. However, cloning should not become a replacement for protecting natural habitats because the animals that are cloned do not need to be living in a cage, just to prove that there is in fact one Gaur left. Every animal plays an important role in its ecosystem and the extinction of one animal, plant or bacteria can disrupt the whole ecosystem.

Lauren Kemp, *Daily Mississippian*, October 19, 2000.

Such creatures increase the gene pool, and if you'll forgive another water image, offer some insurance policy against the flood tide of extinction.

A Gap in Environmental Behavior

But I can't help thinking that while "spindly-legged little Noah" is going up the ramp, about a hundred species are becoming extinct every day.

While a handful of scientists are laboriously applying the most advanced technology to reproduce one endangered creature, people are using the simplest of tools—from a match to a machete—to eliminate habitats of hundreds more.

Indeed, the news bulletin from the frontiers of biotechnology is a reminder of the stunning gap in the environmental behavior of our own species.

On the one hand, a growing, needy, world population eliminates nature day by day.

Meanwhile, a handful of sophisticated scientists works overtime in the lab to imitate what should come naturally.

Changing the Nature of Endangered Species

The new cloning of endangered species raises a host of question about our relationship to nature.

Every environmentalist, including the scientists behind Noah, speak up for the primary importance of saving habitats. But what does it mean to save a species if and when its habitat is being destroyed? Do we save it for life on an Iowa farm? Or a zoo? Or a frozen zoo?

The gaur itself, a one-ton creature of India and South Asia, once hunted for food and sport, is now as threatened as the bamboo jungles and grasslands that were its home.

What kind of a future is there with Bessie?

The last bucardo mountain goat died earlier [in 2000] in Spain, but its cells were frozen. Is it truly "extinct" or just waiting for resurrection?

Can we comfort ourselves with a freezer full of cells as species disappear and the wild itself becomes extinct?

Animals such as elephants and primates exist not only as individuals but as tribes.

They live and learn in their place. Do we change their nature by saving them one at a time? Is a gaur raised by a cow still a gaur?

Oliver Ryder, a geneticist at the San Diego Zoo, also sees the poignancy in the progress. We are watching habitats destroyed and creatures cloned at the same time. But hanging on to hope, he welcomes this birth announcement: "After nature comes back from the brink, people will be grateful."

Maybe so. Maybe the cloning of endangered species is not just a scientific parlor trick. But when Noah takes his first steps in Iowa, think about a much larger ark—the size of a whole planet.

Periodical Bibliography

The following articles have been selected to supplement the diverse views presented in this chapter.

Neil Boyce	"Redesigning Dad," *U.S. News & World Report*, November 5, 2001.
Barry Commoner	"Unraveling the DNA Myth: The Spurious Foundation of Genetic Engineering," *Harper's*, February 2002.
Sally Deneen	"Designer People," *E*, January 2001.
George Dvorsky	"It's About Reproductive Rights, Stupid," July 14, 2003. www.betterhumans.com.
Robert B. Eckhardt	"Releasing the Gene Genie," *World & I*, January 2000.
Economist	"Ingenious Medicine," July 1, 2000.
Thomas Fields-Meyer and Debbie Seaman	"Send In the Clones," *People*, September 8, 2003.
David R. Gergen	"Trouble in Paradise," *U.S. News & World Report*, August 20, 2001.
Stephen Leahy	"Biotech Hope and Hype," *Maclean's*, September 30, 2002.
James Le Fanu	"Blinded by Science," *Human Life Review*, Winter 2001.
Celeste McGovern	"Brave New World," *Report Newsmagazine*, August 20, 2001.
Pat Mooney	"Making Well People 'Better,'" *WorldWatch*, July/August 2002.
Jesse Reynolds	"21st Century Eugenics," *TomPaine.common sense*, June 26, 2003.
Simon Smith	"Making Babies Ain't What It Used to Be," July 21, 2003. www.betterhumans.com.
Luba Vangelova	"True or False? Extinction Is Forever," *Smithsonian*, June 2003.
James D. Watson	"All For the Good: Why Genetic Engineering Must Soldier On," *Time*, January 11, 1999.
Robert A. Weinberg	"Of Clones and Clowns," *Atlantic Monthly*, June 2002.
Janice Wood-Harper	"Embryos and Genetic Testing," *Biological Sciences Review*, May 2000.
Todd Woody	"Should We Clone Fading Species?" *Popular Science*, July 2003.

CHAPTER 2

Is Genetic
Engineering Ethical?

Chapter Preface

One of several ethical questions raised in the genetic engineering controversy is whether individuals should have unrestricted access to the results of their genetic tests. Because people sometimes make life-altering decisions based on the results of genetic tests, some argue that these tests constitute a form of genetic engineering. Many bioethicists believe that the information revealed by genetic tests could harm patients; others argue that people are entitled to make their own medical decisions.

In 1996 oncologists refused to tell Joy Simha, a breast cancer survivor, the outcome of a genetic test she had taken to determine if she carried the breast cancer gene, BRCA1. If the test was positive, she planned to have her remaining breast removed because chances were 50 to 85 percent that the breast cancer would recur. "They kept telling me, 'We really feel that the results could be dangerous if they are revealed to you at the wrong time,'" says Simha. "It was just a very paternalistic attitude," she maintains. Simha took her case to the press. "If I did not want to know the results of my test," she said in a *New York Times Magazine* article, "I would not have given the doctors my blood."

However, many bioethicists believe that revealing the results of genetic tests can harm patients. Francis Collins, director of the Human Genome Project, testified before the Senate in 1996 that the information on the BRCA1 tests could be "toxic." George Annas, director of the Law, Medicine, and Ethics Program at the Boston University Schools of Medicine and Public Health, argues, "Since there is no way to prevent [breast cancer] what good is knowing you will probably get it in the future?" Annas also cites Huntington's disease, a devastating degenerative neurological condition that generally strikes middle-aged adults, as an example of a "toxic" genetic test. According to Annas, "You're going to die this horrible death, and there's nothing you can do about it." Thus, Annas reasons, people should not be informed because the knowledge makes currently healthy people think of themselves as sick.

Not everyone agrees with Annas. Commentators such as

Gregory Stock, the director of the Program on Medicine, Technology, and Society at the University of California at Los Angeles, claims that withholding genetic test results from patients insults their intelligence. Bioethicists who support withholding test results, Stock maintains, have "a lack of faith in the individual." According to journalist Ronald Bailey, patients may have good reasons to want genetic test information:

> Instead of debilitating patients, the results may well give them a chance to shape their lives, careers, and reproductive choices appropriately. A man who learns at age 20 that he will contract the dementia of Huntington's in his mid-40s might decide to lead an entirely different life, skipping the corporate grind for any number of alternatives. Or he might choose not to have children so as not to risk passing on the disease.

Other analysts assert that the knowledge derived from genetic tests can positively influence people's decisions about their health and the health of other family members. The Independent Biotechnology Advisory Council (IBAC) of New Zealand claims:

> Genetic testing can give people the opportunity to make choices affecting their future health—or that of their children. Advance warning of a possible disorder may help with life decisions. These might include more regular check-ups in the case of an increased risk, combined with changes to work or lifestyle to lessen the risk. In some cases it can also provide a signal for other extended family members to have their own tests. They too could make changes to prevent or minimise future health problems.

Simha's doctors relented after her case received attention in the press. Her results were negative, and she did not have another mastectomy. Bailey submits, "Far from having a 'toxic' result, the test actually helped Simha avoid another dangerous and painful procedure." Whether or not doctors have the right to withhold the results of genetic tests from their patients remains controversial. In the following chapter, authors debate other ethical issues in the genetic engineering debate.

> *"The road chosen and driven by compassionate humaneness paved by biotechnology . . . leads not to human fulfillment but to human debasement."*

Genetic Engineering Threatens Human Dignity

Leon R. Kass

In the following viewpoint Leon R. Kass argues that genetic engineering will slowly erode human dignity. According to Kass, blind faith in scientific progress has placed genetic scientists in God-like roles. Indeed, scientists are defining health for the rest of humanity and are even determining which babies will or will not be born. Genetic scientists claim that their goal is to improve human life, but in the pursuit of human perfection through genetic technology, claims Kass, these pseudo-gods will actually destroy what it means to be human. Kass, a physician and professor, is chairman of the President's Council on Bioethics.

As you read, consider the following questions:
1. In Kass's view, what kind of obstetrics will be necessary to produce babies that benefit from genetic enhancement?
2. According to Kass, what will happen to standards of health, wholeness, or fitness with the advent of genetic enhancement?
3. What do genetic engineering enthusiasts fail to see in their utopian project, in the author's opinion?

Leon R. Kass, *Life, Liberty and the Defense of Dignity*. San Francisco: Encounter Books, 2002. Copyright © 2002 by Encounter Books. Reproduced by permission.

Threats to human dignity can—and probably will—arise even with the free, humane, and "enlightened" use of [genetic] technologies. Genetic technology, the practices it will engender, and above all the scientific teachings about human life on which it rests are not, as many would have it, morally and humanly neutral. Regardless of how they are practiced or taught, they are pregnant with their own moral meanings and will necessarily bring with them changes in our practices, our institutions, our norms, our beliefs, and our self-conception. It is, I submit, these challenges to our dignity and humanity that are at the bottom of our anxiety over genetic science and technology. Let me touch briefly on four aspects of this most serious matter.

Playing God

Paradoxically, worries about dehumanization are sometimes expressed in the fear of super humanization, that is, that man will be "playing God." This complaint is too facilely dismissed by scientists and nonbelievers. The concern has meaning, God or no God.

Never mind the exaggeration that lurks in this conceit of man's playing God. (Even at his most powerful, after all, man is capable only of *playing* God.) Never mind the implicit innuendo that nobody has given to others this creative and judgmental authority, or the implicit retort that there is theological warrant for acting as God's co-creator in overcoming the ills and suffering of the world. Consider only that if scientists are seen in this godlike role of creator, judge, and savior, the rest of us must stand before them as supplicating, tainted creatures. Despite the hyperbolic speech, that is worry enough.

Practitioners of prenatal diagnosis, working today with but a fraction of the information soon to be available from the Human Genome Project, already screen for a long list of genetic diseases and abnormalities, from Down syndrome to dwarfism. Possession of any one of these defects, they believe, renders a prospective child unworthy of life. Persons who happen still to be born with these conditions, having somehow escaped the spreading net of detection and eugenic abortion, are increasingly regarded as "mistakes," as inferior human beings who should not have been born. Not long ago, at my own university, a physician making rounds with medical students stood over the bed of an intelligent, otherwise normal ten-year-old boy with spina bifida. "Were he to have been conceived today," the physician casually informed his entourage, "he would have been aborted." Determining who shall live and who shall die—on the basis of genetic merit—is a godlike power already wielded by genetic medicine. This power will only grow.

The Commodification of Human Life

But, one might reply, genetic technology also holds out the promise of redemption, of a *cure* for these life-crippling and life-forfeiting disorders. Very well. But in order truly to practice their salvific power, genetic technologists will have to increase greatly their manipulations and interventions, well beyond merely screening and weeding out. True, in some cases genetic testing and risk management aimed at prevention may actually cut down on the need for high-tech interventions aimed at cure. But in many other cases, ever-greater genetic scrutiny will lead necessarily to ever more extensive manipulation. And, to produce [geneticist] Bentley Glass's [vision of] healthy and well-endowed babies, let alone babies with the benefits of genetic enhancement, a new scientific obstetrics will be necessary, one that will come very close to turning human procreation into manufacture.

This process was already crudely begun with in vitro fertilization. It is now taking giant steps forward with the ability to screen in vitro embryos before implantation (so-called pre-implantation genetic diagnosis). And it will come to maturity with interventions such as cloning and, eventually, with precise genetic engineering. Just follow the logic and the aspirations of current practice: the road we are traveling leads all the way to the world of designer babies—reached not by dictatorial fiat, but by the march of benevolent humanitarianism, and cheered on by an ambivalent citizenry that also dreads becoming merely the last of man's man-made things.

Make no mistake: the price to be paid for producing optimum or even only genetically sound babies will be the transfer of procreation from the home to the laboratory. Such an arrangement will be profoundly dehumanizing, no matter how genetically good or healthy the resultant children. And let us not forget the powerful economic interests that will surely operate in this area; with their advent, the commodification of nascent human life will be unstoppable.

A New Standard of Health

According to Genesis, God, in His creating, looked at His creatures and saw that they were *good*—intact, complete, well-working wholes, true to the spoken idea that guided their creation. What standards will guide the genetic engineers?

For the time being, one might answer, the norm of health. But even before the genetic enhancers join the party, the standard of health is being deconstructed. Are you healthy if, although you show no symptoms, you carry genes that will definitely produce Huntington's disease? What if you carry, say, 40 percent of the genetic markers thought to be linked to the appearance of Alzheimer's disease? And what will "healthy" and "normal" mean when we discover your genetic propensities for alcoholism, drug abuse, pederasty, or violence? The idea of health progressively becomes at once both imperial and vague: medicalization of what have hitherto been mental or moral matters paradoxically brings with it the disappearance of any clear standard of health itself.

Heading for a Caste Society

If . . . the affluent produce genetically enhanced children, the likelihood of them marrying outside their own social, economic and genetic group will vanish and we will be heading for a caste society. This will produce even deeper antagonisms than class-conflict and colour-bars, for we will be creating two radically different groups of human beings—a master race and a servile race. If playing God with genetics is itself immoral, the society it will eventually bring into being will be biologically evil in ways we can scarcely imagine.

Paul Johnson, *Spectator*, March 6, 1999.

Once genetic *enhancement* comes on the scene, standards of health, wholeness, or fitness will be needed more than ever, but just then is when all pretense of standards will go out the window. "Enhancement" is, of course, a euphemism for "improvement," and the idea of improvement necessarily implies a good, a better, and perhaps even a best. If, however, we can no longer look to our previously unalterable human nature for a standard or norm of what is good or better, how will anyone know what constitutes an improvement? It will not do to assert that we can extrapolate from what we like about ourselves. Because memory is good, can we say how much more memory would be better? If sexual desire is good, how much more would be better? Life is good, but how much extension of the life span would be good for us? Only simplistic thinkers believe they can easily answer such questions.

More modest enhancers, like more modest genetic therapists and technologists, eschew grandiose goals. They are valetudinarians, not eugenicists. They pursue not some far away positive good, but the positive elimination of evils: diseases, pain, suffering, the likelihood of death. But let us not be deceived. Hidden in all this avoidance of evil is nothing less than the quasi-messianic goal of a painless, suffering-free and, finally, immortal existence. Only the presence of such a goal justifies the sweeping-aside of any opposition to the relentless march of medical science. Only such a goal gives trumping moral power to the principle "cure disease, relieve suffering."

Justifying Dehumanizing Technologies

"Cloning human beings is unethical and dehumanizing you say? Never mind: it will help us treat infertility, avoid genetic disease, and provide perfect materials for organ replacement." Such, indeed, was the tenor of the June 1997 report of the National Bioethics Advisory Commission, *Cloning Human Beings*. Notwithstanding its call for a temporary ban on the practice, the only moral objection the commission could agree upon was that cloning "is not safe to use in humans at this time," because the technique has yet to be perfected. Even this elite ethical body, in other words, was unable to muster any other moral argument sufficient to cause us to forgo the possible health benefits of cloning.

The same argument will also justify creating and growing human embryos for experimentation, revising the definition of death to increase the supply of organs for transplantation, growing human body parts in the peritoneal cavities of animals, perfusing newly dead bodies as factories for useful biological substances, or reprogramming the human body and mind with genetic or neurobiological engineering. Who can sustain an objection if these practices will help us live longer and with less overt suffering?

It turns out that even the more modest biogenetic engineers, whether they know it or not, are in the immortality business, proceeding on the basis of a quasi-religious faith that all innovation is by definition progress, no matter what is sacrificed to attain it.

The Tragedy of Success

What the enthusiasts do not see is that their utopian project will not eliminate suffering but merely shift it around. Forgetting that contentment requires that our desires do not outpace our powers, they have not noticed that the enormous medical progress of the last half-century has not left the present generation satisfied. Indeed, we are already witnessing a certain measure of public discontent as a paradoxical result of rising expectations in the health care field: although their actual health has improved substantially in recent decades, people's *satisfaction* with their current health status has remained the same or declined. But that is hardly the highest cost of success in the medical/humanitarian project.

As Aldous Huxley made clear in his prophetic *Brave New World*, the road chosen and driven by compassionate humaneness paved by biotechnology, if traveled to the end, leads not to human fulfillment but to human debasement. Perfected bodies are achieved at the price of flattened souls. What Tolstoy called "real life"—life in its immediacy, vividness, and rootedness—has been replaced by an utterly mediated, sterile, and disconnected existence. In one word: dehumanization, the inevitable result of making the essence of human nature the final object of the conquest of nature for the relief of man's estate. Like Midas, bioengineered man will be cursed to acquire precisely what he wished for, only to discover—painfully and too late—that what he wished for is not exactly what he wanted. Or, worse than Midas, he may be so dehumanized he will not even recognize that in aspiring to be perfect, he is no longer even truly human. To paraphrase Bertrand Russell, technological humanitarianism is like a warm bath that heats up so imperceptibly you don't know when to scream.

The main point here is not the rightness or wrongness of this or that imagined scenario; all this is, admittedly, highly speculative. I surely have no way of knowing whether my worst fears will be realized, but you surely have no way of knowing they will not. The point is rather the plausibility, even the wisdom, of thinking about genetic technology like the entire technological venture, under the ancient and profound idea of tragedy in which success and failure are inseparably grown together like the concave and the convex. What I am suggesting is that genetic technology's way of approaching human life, a way spurred on by the utopian promises and perfectionist aims of modern thought and its scientific crusaders, may well turn out to be inevitable, heroic, and doomed. If this suggestion holds water, then the question regarding genetic technology is not "triumph OR tragedy" because the answer is "both together.". . .

Defending Human Dignity

Hence our peculiar moral crisis. We are in turbulent seas without a landmark precisely because we adhere more and more to a view of human life that both gives us enormous power and, *at the same time*, denies every possibility of non arbitrary standards for guiding its use. Though well equipped, we know not who we are or where we are going. We triumph over nature's unpredictability only to subject ourselves, tragically, to the still greater unpredictability of our capricious wills and our fickle opinions. Engineering the engineer as well as the engine, we race our train we know not where. That we do not recognize our predicament is itself a tribute to the depth of our infatuation with scientific progress and our naive faith in the sufficiency of our humanitarian impulses.

Does this mean that I am therefore in favor of ignorance, suffering, and death? Of killing the goose of genetic technology even before she lays her golden eggs? Surely not. But unless we mobilize the courage to look foursquare at the full human meaning of our new enterprise in biogenetic technology and engineering, we are doomed to become its creatures if not its slaves. Important though it is to set a moral boundary here, devise a regulation there, hoping to decrease the damage caused by this or that little rivulet, it is even more important to be sober about the true nature and meaning of the flood itself.

That our exuberant new biologists and their technological minions might be persuaded of this is, to say the least, highly unlikely. For all their ingenuity, they do not even seek the wisdom that just might yield the kind of knowledge that keeps human life human. But it is not too late for the rest of us to become aware of the dangers—not just to privacy or insurability, but to our very humanity. So aware, we might be better able to defend the increasingly beleaguered vestiges and principles of our human dignity, even as we continue to reap the considerable benefits that genetic technology will inevitably provide.

"*Human persons . . . can direct human endeavors in genomics toward ends that contribute to human flourishing and promote truly human values.*"

Genetic Engineering Promotes Human Dignity

Michael Place

Genetic engineering will preserve human dignity as long as genetic scientists respect nature and use their knowledge to serve humanity, claims Michael Place in the following viewpoint. The God-given gifts of reason and creativity have led human beings to genomic knowledge so that they might alleviate human suffering, maintains Place. As long as scientists do not succumb to the sins of pride and greed in their use of genomic knowledge, he argues, the dignity of humanity will be preserved. Place, a priest, is president of the Catholic Health Association of the United States.

As you read, consider the following questions:
1. According to Place, what is the harrowing task before all who will be touched by genomic technology?
2. What position in the created order do human beings hold as a result of the gifts they have been given, in the author's view?
3. In the author's opinion, where does sin originate and how is it expressed?

S ome think we should avoid any involvement in genomics because it implicates us in "playing God" "altering nature," "violating human dignity" and "undermining the common good." These are serious and legitimate concerns. We know all too well that hubris and other human passions can divert our efforts from ethically acceptable ends. Sometimes even the best of intentions can lead to harm. Nevertheless, this does not necessarily mean that we must turn away from the promise of genomics. The issue is much more nuanced and complex than that.

A Theological Vision

Along with the possibility of causing harm, there is also the opportunity to improve the health of those living with many genetic diseases and thereby eliminate or alleviate the pain and suffering that so often accompany them. In fact the knowledge about the human genome, the translation of that knowledge into various diagnostic and therapeutic measures, and the just application of those measures to persons afflicted by disease can be a response to our call to participate in God's creative and healing work in the world. These activities can provide us with opportunities for living out in part what it means to be created in the image of God and continuing the healing ministry of Jesus for the advancement of the reign of God. Viewed in this light, we should embrace the promise of genomics but must do so with constant vigilance. The harrowing task before all of us who will inevitably be touched by genomic technologies—whether genetic testing, pharmacogenetics or eventually gene therapy—is and will be to harness that promise and avoid the perils as much as possible.

Where do we look for the wisdom to chart the delicate course between the promise and the peril of genomics? What is at stake after all is not just the pursuit of genomic research, the development and use of certain genomic technologies, and the potential relief of human suffering, but more important, some of the most basic aspects of what it means to be human. Though there are many possible sources to which we might turn for wisdom, from a Catholic-Christian perspective we look to Scripture, tradition, reason and experience. Within these sources we find a theological vision that can shed light on advances in genomics. The . . . vision consists of relevant theological themes—human creativity, human finitude, and sin and grace—that can shape our relationship to human endeavors in genomics more generally. . . .

The Gift of Human Creativity

The created world that was gifted to us by God out of love is laden with potential waiting to be unleashed and brought to ever fuller realization. As human beings with a spiritual nature, we have been privileged with reason and will, freedom and responsibility, and imagination and creativity. We have been gifted with the powers to understand our own selves and the world around us, and to make use of this knowledge in the service of humanity and the created world itself. Hence, science as an exercise of human intelligence is a valued and valid enterprise and part of what it means to "image God." The Second Vatican Council and Pope John Paul II in particular have said as much by affirming the distinctive vocation of the sciences and the autonomy that should be accorded to them. Yet they are also clear that science must always contribute to the integral well-being of humanity and must always respect creation, never seeking to be masters over it but only stewards of it. From this it follows that not all that can be done scientifically ought to be done, that at times we may need to bypass or limit our use of some genomic advances because of higher, more important goods at stake.

Because of the gifts we have been given, human beings hold a position of great responsibility within the created order. We are charged with participating in the unfolding of creation and making visible God's love of creation. Yet despite the unique standing of human beings vis-à-vis creation, the created world did not come to be merely for human use. Rather, it is an external manifestation of God's love and goodness, and is ultimately oriented toward participation in the fullness of divine life. Creation is born of God's love and is directed back to that love as its final goal. Though we have a role as human beings in bringing about the transformation of creation toward greater life and wholeness, only God affects the final and complete transformation. Partial realizations of it may exist now. However, it is ultimately God's gra-

The Promise of Biotechnology

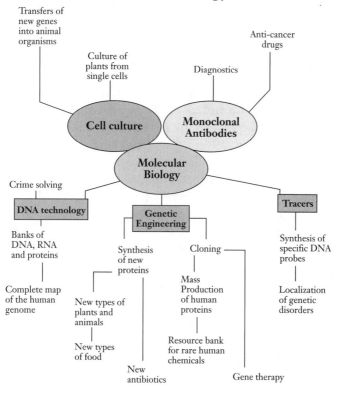

Transfers of new genes into animal organisms

Culture of plants from single cells

Diagnostics

Anti-cancer drugs

Cell culture

Monoclonal Antibodies

Molecular Biology

Crime solving

DNA technology

Genetic Engineering

Tracers

Banks of DNA, RNA and proteins

Synthesis of new proteins

Cloning

Synthesis of specific DNA probes

Complete map of the human genome

New types of plants and animals

Mass Production of human proteins

Localization of genetic disorders

New types of food

Resource bank for rare human chemicals

New antibiotics

Gene therapy

Access Excellence at the National Health Museum, 1999.

cious gift beyond human history. Recognizing that the fulfillment of creation is ultimately a gift of God can help us temper unrealistic expectations about human endeavors in genomics and can enable us to use our freedom and creativity toward ends that promote human flourishing and respect creation.

The Limits of Human Endeavors

Human beings have come into existence, as has all of creation, as an expression of God's creative love. Although made in God's image, we are not God. We are physical beings immersed in the material world and thus finite. Finitude is an integral part of human existence, and as such we will always be defined by and have to live with limitation.

This is what it means to be creature and not God. We can and should strive to overcome some of the limitations we experience, but a complete transcendence of every limitation will never be possible.

While we seek to improve the human condition and even have an obligation to do so, we must always be cognizant of the fact that it will never be perfect. We will never be able to eliminate all disease and disability and the suffering that results from them. Nor will the reduction of disease, disability or suffering by themselves bring about happiness and human flourishing. Human endeavors in genomics need to be viewed against the backdrop of our ultimate finitude, which suggests perfection of the genome is an elusive goal and we will have to accept some limits even while trying to transcend the limitations imposed by genetic mutations through our ability to give them meaning.

The Phenomena of Sin and Grace

As we so well know, human beings do not always pursue ends that are truly meaningful and often exceed ethical limits. Human intelligence, free choice and creative powers are not always used to promote God's good creation and human flourishing. From the beginning, we have abused our capacities, especially our freedom, to pursue ends harmful and even destructive of our relationships with ourselves, others, God and creation. Pride, egocentrism, greed, ambition and other false gods tend to distort the ends that are most fitting for human beings to pursue. This phenomenon that we call *sin* originates in the disordered desires and choices of individuals. In many cases it is expressed and even embodied in social attitudes, policies and structures. The effects of sin are part of the context in which individual human choices are made. Sin is an ever present reality and danger in the attempt to achieve a more complete understanding of the human genome. What is more, sin can infect the development and use of genomic applications and divert these goods from their proper goal of contributing to human flourishing.

Yet while sin is an ever present danger and potent force, it is not the last word. Where sin abounds, grace abounds even more. Grace, God's free and unmerited self-offer that enables humans to share in the divine life, is also ever present and a supremely more potent force. Through grace, humanity and all of creation are invited to enter into the fullness of communion with God. Grace is a sign that God loves all human beings despite sin and enables human freedom to move in the direction of self-transcending love as a response to God's initiative of love and call to be loving. Grace, too, is part of the context in which individual human choices are made and can also become embodied in social attitudes, policies and structures insofar as they contribute to transformation for the reign of God. By responding to grace, human persons can minimize the effects of sin bound up in hubris and the desire to master nature, and as such can direct human endeavors in genomics toward ends that contribute to human flourishing and promote truly human values.

"There is widespread abhorrence at the thought of reproductive cloning . . . . Therapeutic cloning is [also] dangerous and should be banned."

Human Cloning Is Unethical

Megan Best

According to Megan Best in the following viewpoint, all human cloning is unethical. While there is widespread agreement that human reproductive cloning, in which replicas of whole organisms are made, should be banned, less debate surrounds therapeutic cloning, used to create healthy cells to replace damaged ones in sick people, she argues. Because patients' bodies will reject incompatible stem cells, claims Best, researchers will inevitably have to create embryonic clones of patients. These clones, she argues, will be killed when their cells are harvested for injection into the patient, which is unethical. It is always wrong to sacrifice one life for the benefit of another, she contends. Best is a medical doctor, bioethicist, and member of the Social Issues Executive of the Anglican Media of Sydney, Australia.

As you read, consider the following questions:

1. In Best's opinion, how should frozen embryos currently in storage be treated?
2. According to Best, why are IVF [in vitro fertilization] embryos unsuitable for the stage of stem-cell therapy in which stem cells are transformed into the required cell type and injected into patients?
3. Why will therapeutic cloning lead to the exploitation of women, in the author's opinion?

W hile Australian media has been enthusiastic in its support of the benefits of embryonic stem cell research,
. . . it has not always spelt out the route by which such research would yield therapeutic benefits. This paper will explain why human cloning is required for the full therapeutic
benefits of embryonic stem cell research to be realised and
why it is unethical.

Treating Frozen Embryos with Dignity

Approximately 70,000 frozen embryos are currently in storage after implantation has been ruled out for them in assisted reproductive procedures such as IVF [in vitro fertil-
ization]. We have been encouraged to support the use of
these so-called 'spare' embryos for stem cell harvest. Such a
procedure will kill the embryo involved, but it has been suggested that this is a small price to pay for the proposed scientific benefits.

We suggest that human embryos should not be the subjects of experimental research aimed at benefiting someone
other than the embryos themselves. We believe that human
embryos are just that, human. Therefore they should be
given the chance of life through adoption to infertile couples, or allowed to die with the respect due to their humanity. While not all Australians agree on the moral status of the
embryo, most agree that it is worthy of respect and dignity,
as is suggested by the resources currently invested in the
storage of the embryos in question.

We also object to development of embryonic stem cell research because of the implicit endorsement of human
cloning involved.

Cloning in Embryonic Stem Cell Research

If destructive research is allowed, embryonic stem cells will
be extracted and grown as cell lines for research. These cells
can reproduce indefinitely. The aim will be to refine the
procedures which can direct and control the metamorphosis
of stem cells into other body tissues.

While stem cell lines may be useful in themselves for research in areas such as pharmaceutical treatments, the therapeutic goal as presented by proponents of embryonic stem

cell research is much more ambitious. With the development of procedures to push stem cells into various tissue pathways, it is suggested that we will be able to inject specific cells into patients to replace malfunctioning or absent cells. For example, nerve cells may mend a severed spinal cord, insulin-producing cells may cure a diabetic.

Kauffmann. © 2001 by Joel Kauffmann. Reproduced by permission.

However, should the methods required to control these transformations be understood, in order to inject stem cells into a human subject, the problem of rejection by the body's immune system needs to be overcome. In order to make stem cells compatible with a patient, it is proposed that a human clone of the patient be created and grown to approximately 6 day stage, at which time the stem cells will be harvested and therefore the embryo killed. The stem cells will be transformed into the required cell type before injection into the patient. The stem cells harvested from IVF embryos will not be suitable for this stage of treatment as they will have different genetic makeup from the patient, and if injected will therefore be identified by the body as foreign and attacked by the immune system, probably rendering them useless. While some biotechnology companies have allegedly considered alternative methods of genetic engineering to overcome the immune rejection, nothing has been published on this subject.

A Dangerous Distinction

The procedure used to create a patient clone will be somatic cell nuclear transfer—the method used to create Dolly the sheep. A body cell other than an egg or sperm will have its nucleus removed. That nucleus will be placed in a human egg which has had its nucleus removed. This egg is then subjected to electrical impulses which will stimulate growth of the embryo.

Prior to actual treatment of patients, it is probable that scientists will want to clone humans by this technique to allow the improvement of the cloning procedure before patient trials begin.

The [November 2001] announcement that an American biotechnology company, Advanced Cell Technology, had created the first cloned human was received with alarm by the Australian public. While scientists have attempted to alleviate these concerns by distinguishing 'therapeutic' from 'reproductive' cloning, we believe that this terminology is unhelpful. While there is widespread abhorrence at the thought of reproductive cloning, the public has been told that therapeutic cloning holds no such risks. We believe that therapeutic cloning is dangerous and should be banned along with reproductive cloning for the following reasons.

Why 'Therapeutic' Human Cloning Is Unethical

1. Therapeutic cloning can only be justified by the utilitarian calculus that values potential medical treatments over the lives of the embryos who would be destroyed in order for the research to proceed. However it is not ethical to sacrifice one human life for the real or potential benefit of others.

2. It is unethical to view a human being—regardless of its age—as a means to an end. Creation of human embryos specifically for destructive research is opposed by our community, and this is what is involved in therapeutic cloning.

3. Therapeutic cloning will undoubtedly lead to exploitation of women. In order to create human clones for stem cell therapy, an enormous number of women's eggs will need to be donated. To do so, women may be treated with superovulatory drugs and must undergo an invasive procedure. Complications may occur. Advanced Cell Technology paid up to $4,000 to each woman who donated eggs for their cloning experiments. It is likely that women of lower economic status will be exploited in this way.

4. In addition to the ethical concerns above, therapeutic cloning should be banned because it increases the likelihood of reproductive cloning. Preventing the implanting and subsequent birth of cloned embryos once they are available in the laboratory will be impossible. Already Dr Severino Antinori of Italy has plans to produce the first cloned human. The most effective way to prevent reproductive cloning is to stop the process at the beginning, with the creation of cloned embryos. Since the overwhelming community consensus is that reproductive cloning should be banned, steps must be taken to ban therapeutic cloning as well.

Embryonic stem cell research and therapeutic cloning should also be banned in view of the existence of other promising and ethical treatment options such as adult stem cell therapy (which has already been successfully used in patients).

In conclusion, if destruction of excess embryos is allowed, does this just apply to the embryos currently in storage, or to future 'excess' embryos as well? The blatant irresponsibility of IVF clinics that have allowed the accumulation of approximately 70,000 embryos to date will have no incentive to change if future excess embryos are also fodder for the laboratory.

"Our ability to clone humans . . . would be far more ethical than many people believe."

Human Cloning Is Ethical

Stuart K. Hayashi

In the following viewpoint Stuart K. Hayashi argues that claims against cloning are based on the misconception that human clones would be exact duplicates of adults. In reality, clones will grow up in unique environments, exercise free will, and develop their own personalities, Hayashi contends. Cloning human embryos to produce new medicines is also an ethical use of biotechnology, he claims, because of the enormous advantages such procedures would convey. Hayashi is a research intern at the Grassroot Institute of Hawaii, an organization whose goal is to foster free-market philosophy.

As you read, consider the following questions:

1. How does Hayashi answer the claim that clones will be treated as outcasts because they will grow up in households different from the socially accepted norm?
2. In the author's opinion, how do individual rights protect clones from abuse?
3. According to Hayashi, how will cloning give psychologists a better understanding of which factors develop our character the most?

S ince the dawn of time, there were those who opposed mankind's ventures into then-uncharted scientific frontiers—anesthesia, nuclear energy, and computer technology—out of fear of the changes in everyday life they would invoke. Today, such is the case with our ability to clone humans for reproductive purposes, which would be far more ethical than many people believe. The attempts to permanently ban human cloning should not succeed, because it has been fueled by misconception, is a violation of individual property rights, and will be of great detriment to society in the future.

First, this author should clarify that he is not eager to see someone succeed in implanting any cloned human embryos into anyone in the near future, due to the imperfection that exists in current cloning techniques. Many cloned animal embryos have self-aborted, and Dolly the now-deceased sheep clone aged at a rate faster than a non-cloned sheep would have. However, assuming that scientists could finally learn to clone humans, without these defects popping up, there would cease to be any credible moral objections to cloning.

While so many people declare that to clone a human being for reproductive purposes would be innately immoral, even if the clone were healthy, few of these individuals have an accurate idea of what cloning truly is. It is commonly believed that a clone of an adult will be an exact duplicate, down to the very age and personality of the *clonee* (what this author calls the genetic parent of a clone; i.e., if John is a clone made from Todd's genetic material, then Todd is the *clonee*). In reality, however, all clones must start off as babies and, if the problems with Dolly's premature aging are corrected in future cloning techniques, they will physically mature at the same rate as everyone else. Thus, if one clones a thirty-year-old man, the clone will always appear thirty years younger than the original.

Another erroneous belief is that the clone will behave exactly like the clonee, thereby robbing the original of his or her uniqueness. Self-proclaimed "bioethicists" often create a fictitious scenario in which someone clones Hitler and takes over the world. What these arguments ignore is that individual personality is largely shaped by environment, conditioning, and free will, and *not* just by biology.

If life experiences and background truly mold a person's character, then these circumstances must be taken into account for the personalities of clones. Being born in a different time period, the clone will already face many life experiences unlike that of the parent—he will have different friends, be influenced by different teachers, and adapt to the modern culture of his own age group. This already creates vast variations between the clone and his or her parent. Also vital is how the clone is raised. His legal guardians may bring him up with different values and beliefs than the clonee, and may discipline him in ways unlike that of the original's parents. As Stanford University economist Thomas Sowell noted, "If a Rush Limbaugh clone turns out to be a liberal or a Bill Clinton clone turns out to be honest, this could shatter the grand illusion of [genetic] determinism and all the foolish policies based on that illusion."

Even more important than either environment or conditioning, it should be added, is free will. Every individual, regardless of his or her genetic code, must decide for him- or herself how he or she will behave. Though identical twins share the same DNA structure, and were born in the same time period and raised in the very same environment with the same conditioning, they are still individual, autonomous entities who live and think independently of one another. Though they are nature's own clones, a few twins even turn out to be behavioral opposites. A clone of Hitler may end up a freedom-espousing, *Civil Rights* advocate. While cloning may be possible in the near future, exact duplication remains a simple pipedream. Any "egotist" or would-be dictator who expects his clone to be an exact copy of himself will be sorely disappointed.

One of the more valid issues raised by bioethicists is that the pioneering clones will grow up in households different from the socially-accepted norm, and that they may be treated as outcasts. However, today children are growing up in many different households considered less than ideal, such as single-parent homes or families with *in-vitro* fertilized children. Though these households were once regarded as abnormal, most of the children in them mature into well-adjusted adults who function satisfactorily in the community. Their situation differing from that of the status quo did not fully impede their development. Also, over time, the more clones are made, the more society will grow accustomed to them.

There are indeed many more serious issues involving clones not raised by the bioethicists, but all of these can be answered by applying the principles of individual property rights. If Americans truly have a right to their own life and liberty, then surely they own their own unique genetic code. Also, because one owns his own physiological structure, he should have the right to peacefully do whatever he wants with it—such as cloning himself—provided that he does not harm the life, liberty, or property of others. Just as a couple has a right to have children when, where, and how they see fit, so too does a person who wishes to have a child-clone. Forbidding a man to clone himself, because we perceive him to be irresponsible, would be like forbidding a poor, young, unmarried couple to have children simply because we perceive *them* as not being responsible enough.

An Impartial Discussion of Cloning Is Difficult

[Cloning is] just a tool, just another way to create a family. A long legacy in science fiction novels and movies make the word "cloning" so fraught with bad connotations that it can hardly be used in any discussion that purports to be impartial. It is like discussing equal rights for women by starting to discuss whether "the chicks" would fare better with equal rights. To most people, "cloning" implies selfish parents, crazy scientists, and out-of-control technology, so a fair discussion using this word isn't possible. Perhaps the phrase, "somatic cell nuclear transplantation" is better, even if it's a scientific mouthful. So if we shouldn't call a person created by cloning, a "clone," what should we call him? Answer: a person.

Gregory E. Pence, 2001.

Still, one question this raises is, "If cloning is legal, what should stop 'mad scientists' from cloning *others* against their will?" The answer is that, since an individual owns his or her own DNA, no one can use his or her genetic material for any purpose other than what he or she permits, just as it is illegal to publicly use another's likeness without his or her consent.

Individual rights also protect clones from abuse. Full-bodied, human clones would have rights, because, unlike animals and separately-cloned body parts, they have the ability to think, which means that they possess the abstract concept of rights, and can therefore adhere to the rights of others (if animals had rights, then that means that lions would have to go to prison for "murder" whenever they followed their naturally-evolved, inborn instinct to kill zebras). Because of this, it would be illegal to grow an *entire body* for transplanting body parts, since this violates the clone's rights to life and liberty.

One may still worry that, if clones were accepted into everyday life, the dreadful scenario of the novel *Brave New World* may be brought to reality. The story focuses on a civilization of clones whose lives are identical, and who are easily ruled by a totalitarian elite. The subjects possessing the same genetic code makes them more likely to agree with one another and conform. However, when discussing this frightening, hypothetical situation, a number of things must be pointed out—besides its being only fiction. A society like the one in the book is made possible only by the absolute, arbitrary rule of the government which has the power to decide everything for everyone, from cradle to grave. *Brave New World*'s technocratic politicians are not capitalistic, but semi-fascist, semi-socialist, and have gained their power only because their citizens chose collectivism and central State planning over individual choice and limited government. The situation presented in the story cannot be brought to fruition under America's free enterprise system, because individuals can choose for themselves what they want to do with their own lives. People can choose whether or not they want themselves cloned, and even clones have the option of having children by more natural, socially-accepted means. Anyone, clone or non-clone, can associate with anyone they choose—clone or non-clone—for any reason whatsoever. The State can only control the lives of individuals if the electorate unwittingly gives it this power. In order to avoid creating a civilization like the one in *Brave New World*, what must be opposed is not technological progress, but the government's growing power to regulate what we do with our own minds, bodies, and belongings. As long as our system of free exchange and private property are preserved, human cloning will not threaten society, but benefit it enormously.

The cloning of human beings in the future will improve life in a number of ways. The mere cloning of human embryos, which will not even develop into fetuses, can be used in the production of new medicines. (This use is not a violation of life, since the embryo has not become a true human being, as many abortion rights activists may note).

Also, the cloning of existing adults will give psychologists a better understanding of which factors develop our character *the most*. For years, psychologists of various intellectual schools have argued over what is most important in making us who we are—biology, environment, conditioning, chance, or free will? Should clones behave differently from their parents, it will *show once and for all* that physiological makeup *does not* shape our destiny. If a Rush Limbaugh clone *really were* raised by liberal foster parents and came out a liberal himself, that would support the case of the "Behaviorist" school of psychology—founded by the likes of the late B.F. Skinner of Harvard University—which insists on the importance of conditioning. However, if a man reared his own clone in a manner very similar to his own upbringing and the clone still turned out different, it would finally *prove* the supremacy of free will over both conditioning and physiology.

Human cloning would probably most improve life for infertile couples who would still like to have biological children. Many of these couples would prefer to have babies by more natural, socially-accepted means, but this is simply not an option for them. They still desire to pass on their own genes to *another* generation, however, and cloning makes this possible. Any infertile couple who disapproves of this scientific breakthrough will still be able to adopt. While people exercising their own right to peacefully use their own DNA as they see fit *do not* infringe on our rights in any way, the way *we* treat *them* is a different story! Does our fear of the unknown, and intolerance for those who are different, justify *denying* infertile couples the joys of raising their own biological children?!

It is natural for humans to fear the new and unusual, but when we let this fear control us, we may refuse ourselves great pleasures and prosperity. Not only does real human cloning contradict the misconceptions we have formed, but abuses in this area would be most adequately controlled by are already-established free market system, and the advancements made in our civilization would be fantastic. A ban would undermine *all of this*. Rather than cling to the status quo and equilibrium of everyday life, we would do well to put our prejudices aside, and welcome the grand wonders and joys human cloning will bestow upon the world.

"Is it ethically justifiable to pursue
[genetically modified] crops and foods?
. . . *The answer is yes.*"

The Production of Genetically Engineered Food Is Ethical

Gary Comstock

In the following viewpoint Gary Comstock asserts that ethical claims against genetically modified (GM) foods are not sound. For example, Comstock argues, the claim that producing GM foods is playing God fails to consider that according to some religions, God approves of science and other human endeavors because they improve the human condition. Moreover, according to Comstock, genetically modifying crops is little different from other long-accepted agricultural practices. Comstock is the coordinator of the bioethics program at Iowa State University.

As you read, consider the following questions:
1. According to Comstock, why is it counterintuitive to judge an action wrong simply because it has never been performed?
2. In the author's opinion, why can the principle that biotech commodifies life not be applied uniformly?
3. What different questions do religion and ethics answer, in Comstock's view?

M uch the food consumed in the United States is genetically modified (GM). GM food derives from microorganisms, plants, or animals manipulated at the molecular level to have traits that farmers or consumers desire. These foods often have been produced by techniques in which "foreign" genes are inserted into the microorganisms, plants, or animals. Foreign genes are genes taken from sources other than the organism's natural parents. In other words, GM plants contain genes they would not have contained if researchers had used only traditional plant breeding methods.

Some consumer advocates object to GM foods, and sometimes they object on ethical grounds. When people oppose GM foods on ethical grounds, they typically have some reason for their opposition. We can scrutinize their reasons and, when we do so, we are doing applied ethics. Applied ethics involves identifying peoples' arguments for various conclusions and then analyzing those arguments to determine whether the arguments support their conclusions. A critical goal here is to decide whether an argument is sound. A sound argument is one in which all the premises are true and no mistakes have been made in reasoning. . . .

Discussions of the ethical dimensions of agricultural biotechnology are sometimes confused by a conflation of two quite different sorts of objections to GM technology: intrinsic and extrinsic. It is critical not only that we distinguish these two classes but that we keep them distinct throughout the ensuing discussion of ethics.

The Extrinsic Objections

Extrinsic objections focus on the potential harms consequent upon the adoption of GM organisms (GMOs). Extrinsic objections hold that GM technology should not be pursued because of its anticipated results. Briefly stated, the extrinsic objections go as follows. GMOs may have disastrous effects on animals, ecosystems, and humans. Possible harms to humans include perpetuation of social inequities in modern agriculture, decreased food security for women and children on subsistence farms in developing countries, a growing gap between well-capitalized economies in the northern hemisphere and less capitalized peasant economies in the South, risks to the food security of future generations, and the promotion of reductionistic and exploitative science. Potential harms to ecosystems include possible environmental catastrophe; inevitable narrowing of germplasm diversity; and irreversible loss or degradation of air, soils, and waters. Potential harms to animals include unjustified pain to individuals used in research and production.

These are valid concerns, and nation-states must have in place testing mechanisms and regulatory agencies to assess the likelihood, scope, and distribution of potential harms through a rigorous and well-funded risk assessment procedure. It is for this reason that . . . GM technology must be developed responsibly and with appropriate caution. However, these extrinsic objections cannot by themselves justify a moratorium, much less a permanent ban, on GM technology, because they admit the possibility that the harms may be minimal and outweighed by the benefits. How can one decide whether the potential harms outweigh potential benefits unless one conducts the research, field tests, and data analysis necessary to make a scientifically informed assessment?

In sum, extrinsic objections to GMOs raise important questions about GMOs, and each country using GMOs ought to have in place the organizations and research structures necessary to ensure their safe use.

There is, however, an entirely different sort of objection to GM technology, a sort of objection that, if it is sound, would justify a permanent ban.

The Intrinsic Objections

Intrinsic objections allege that the process of making GMOs is objectionable *in itself*. This belief is defended in several ways, but almost all the formulations are related to one central claim, the unnaturalness objection:

> It is unnatural to genetically engineer plants, animals, and foods. (UE).

If UE is true, then we ought not to engage in bioengineering, however unfortunate may be the consequences of halting the technology. Were a nation to accept UE as the conclusion of a sound argument, then much agricultural research would have to be terminated and potentially significant benefits from the technology sacrificed. A great deal is at stake.

In Comstock, *Vexing Nature? On Ethical Case Against Agricultural Biotechnology*, I discuss 14 ways in which UE has been defended. For present purposes, those 14 objections can be summarized as follows:

(i) To engage in ag biotech is to *play God*.

(ii) To engage in ag biotech is to *invent world-changing technology*.

(iii) To engage in ag biotech is *illegitimately to cross species boundaries*.

(iv) To engage in ag biotech is to *commodify life*.

Let us consider each claim in turn.

Playing God

(i) To engage in ag biotech is to *play God*.

In a western theological framework, humans are creatures, subjects of the Lord of the Universe, and it would be impious for them to arrogate to themselves roles and powers appropriate only for the Creator. Shifting genes around between individuals and species is taking on a task not appropriate for us, subordinate beings. Therefore, to engage in bioengineering is to play God.

There are several problems with this argument. First, there are different interpretations of God. Absent the guidance of any specific religious tradition, it is logically possible that God could be a Being who wants to turn over to us all divine prerogatives, or explicitly wants to turn over to us at least the prerogative of engineering plants, or who doesn't care what we do. If God is any of these beings, then the argument fails because playing God in this instance is not a bad thing.

The argument seems to assume, however, that God is not like any of the gods just described. Assume that the orthodox Jewish and Christian view of God is correct, that God is the only personal, perfect, necessarily existing, all-loving, all-knowing, and all-powerful being. On this traditional western theistic view, finite humans should not aspire to infinite knowledge and power. To the extent that bioengineering is an attempt to control nature itself, the argument would go, bioengineering would be an unacceptable attempt to usurp God's dominion.

Humans Are Co-Creators

The problem with this argument is that not all traditional Jews and Christians think this God would rule out genetic engineering. I am a practicing evangelical Christian and the chair of my local church's council. In my tradition, God is thought to endorse creativity and scientific and technological development, including genetic improvement. Other traditions have similar views. In the mystical writings of the Jewish Kabbalah, God is understood as One who expects humans to be co-creators, technicians working with God to improve the world. At least one Jewish philosopher, Baruch Brody, has suggested that biotechnology may be a vehicle ordained by God for the perfection of nature.

I personally hesitate to think that humans can perfect nature. However, I have become convinced that GM might help humans to rectify some of the damage we have already done to nature. And I believe God may endorse such an aim. For humans are made in the divine image. God desires that we exercise the spark of divinity within us. Inquisitiveness in science is part of our nature. Creative impulses are not found only in the literary, musical, and plastic arts. They are part of molecular biology, cellular theory, ecology, and evolutionary genetics, too. It is unclear why the desire to investigate and manipulate the chemical bases of life should not be considered as much a manifestation of our god-like nature as the writing of poetry and the composition of sonatas. As a way of providing theological content for UE, then, argument (i) is unsatisfactory because it is ambiguous and contentious.

Changing the World

(ii) To engage in ag biotech is to *invent world-changing technology*, an activity that should be reserved to God alone.

Let us consider (ii) in conjunction with a similar objection (iia).

(iia) To engage in ag biotech is to *arrogate historically unprecedented power* to ourselves.

The argument here is not the strong one, that biotech gives us divine power, but the more modest one, that it gives us a power we have not had previously. But it would be counterintuitive to judge an action wrong simply because it has never been performed. On this view, it would have been wrong to prescribe a new herbal remedy for menstrual cramps or to administer a new anesthetic. But that seems absurd. More argumentation is needed to call historically unprecedented actions morally wrong. What is needed is to know *to what extent* our new powers will transform society, whether we have witnessed prior transformations of this sort, and whether those transitions are morally acceptable.

We do not know how extensive the ag biotech revolution will be, but let us assume that it will be as dramatic as its greatest proponents assert. Have we ever witnessed comparable transitions?

A Commitment to Ethical Principles

We develop our agricultural products to enhance the world's food supply and to promote sustainable agriculture with attendant environmental benefits. There are significant advantages to increasing the yield of crops. Farmers must produce increasing amounts of food per acre to feed a growing global population. We will strive to make this possible while reducing the amount of external supplements (fertilizers, pesticides, etc.) necessary. We will develop our products with an eye toward good stewardship of our agricultural and environmental resources and the sustainability of such development. With regard to the development of new agriculture crops, we pledge to abide by established standards of environmental safety at home and abroad.

Biotechnology Industry Organization, 2003.

The change from hunting and gathering to agriculture was an astonishing transformation. With agriculture came not only an increase in the number of humans on the globe but the first appearance of complex cultural activities: writing, philosophy, government, music, the arts, and architecture. What sort of power did people arrogate to themselves when they moved from hunting and gathering to agriculture? The power of civilization itself.

Ag biotech is often oversold by its proponents. But suppose they are right, that ag biotech brings us historically unprecedented powers. Is this a reason to oppose it? Not if we accept agriculture and its accompanying advances, for when

we accepted agriculture we arrogated to ourselves historically unprecedented powers.

In sum, the objections stated in (ii) and (iia) are not convincing.

Crossing Species Boundaries

(iii) To engage in ag biotech is *illegitimately to cross species
boundaries.*

The problems with this argument are both theological and
scientific. I will leave it to others to argue the scientific case
that nature gives ample evidence of generally fluid boundaries between species. The argument assumes that species
boundaries are distinct, rigid, and unchanging, but, in fact,
species now appear to be messy, plastic, and mutable. To
proscribe the crossing of species borders on the grounds that
it is unnatural seems scientifically indefensible.

It is also difficult to see how (iii) could be defended on
theological grounds. None of the scriptural writings of the
western religions proscribes genetic engineering, of course,
because genetic engineering was undreamt of when the holy
books were written. Now, one might argue that such a pro-
scription may be derived from Jewish or Christian traditions
of scriptural interpretation. Talmudic laws against mixing
"kinds," for example, might be taken to ground a general
prohibition against inserting genes from "unclean" species
into clean species. Here's one way the argument might go:
For an observant Jew to do what scripture proscribes is
morally wrong; Jewish oral and written law proscribe the
mixing of kinds (eating milk and meat from the same plate;
yoking donkeys and oxen together); bioengineering is the
mixing of kinds; therefore, for a Jew to engage in bioengineering is morally wrong.

But this argument fails to show that bioengineering is intrinsically objectionable in all its forms for everyone. The argument might prohibit *Jews* from engaging in certain *kinds*
of biotechnical activity but not all; it would not prohibit, for
example, the transferring of genes *within* a species, nor, apparently, the transfer of genes from one clean species to another clean species. Incidentally, it is worth noting that the
Orthodox community has accepted transgenesis in its food

supply. Seventy percent of cheese produced in the United States is made with a GM product, chymosin. This cheese has been accepted as kosher by Orthodox rabbis.

In conclusion, it is difficult to find a persuasive defense of (iii) on either scientific or religious grounds.

The Commodification of Life

(iv) To engage in ag biotech is to *commodify life.*

The argument here is that genetic engineering treats life in a reductionistic manner, reducing living organisms to little more than machines. Life is sacred and not to be treated as a good of commercial value only to be bought and sold to the highest bidder.

Could we apply this principle uniformly? Would not objecting to the products of GM technology on these grounds also require that we object to the products of ordinary agriculture on the same grounds? Is not the very act of bartering or exchanging crops and animals for cash vivid testimony to the fact that every culture on earth has engaged in the commodification of life for centuries? If one accepts commercial trafficking in non-GM wheat and pigs, then why object to commercial trafficking in GM wheat and GM pigs? Why should it be wrong to treat DNA the way we have previously treated animals, plants, and viruses?

Although (iv) may be true, it is not a sufficient reason to object to GM technology because our values and economic institutions have long accepted the commodification of life. Now, one might object that various religious traditions have never accepted commodification and that genetic engineering presents us with an opportunity to resist, to reverse course. [L.] Kass, for example, has argued that we have gone too far down the road of dehumanizing ourselves and treating nature as a machine and that we should pay attention to our emotional reactions against practices such as human cloning. Even if we cannot defend these feelings in rational terms, our revulsion at the very idea of cloning humans should carry great weight. [M.] Midgley has argued that moving genes across species boundaries is not only "yukky" but, perhaps, a monstrous idea, a form of playing God.

Kass and Midgley have eloquently defended the relevance

of our emotional reactions to genetic engineering but, as both admit, we cannot simply allow our emotions to carry the day. As Midgley writes, "Attention to . . . sympathetic feelings [can stir] up reasoning that [alters] people's whole world view." But as much hinges on the reasoning as on the emotions.

The Problem of Naive Consequentialism

Are the intrinsic objections sound? Are they clear, consistent, and logical? Do they rely on principles we are willing to apply uniformly to other parts of our lives? Might they lead to counterintuitive results?

Counterintuitive results are results we strongly hesitate to accept because they run counter to widely shared considered moral intuitions. If a moral rule or principle leads to counterintuitive results, then we have a strong reason to reject it. For example, consider the following moral principle, which we might call the doctrine of naive consequentialism (NC):

Always improve the welfare of the most people (NC).

Were we to adopt NC, then we would be not only permitted but required to sacrifice one healthy person if by doing so we could save many others. If six people need organ transplants (two need kidneys, one needs a liver, one needs a heart, and two need lungs) then NC instructs us to sacrifice the life of the healthy person to transplant six organs to the other six. But this result, that we are *obliged* to sacrifice innocent people to save strangers, is wildly counterintuitive. This result gives us a strong reason to reject NC.

I have argued that the four formulations of the unnaturalness objection considered above are unsound insofar as they lead to counterintuitive results. I do not take this position lightly. Twelve years ago, I wrote "The Case Against bGH," an article, I have been told, that "was one of the first papers by a philosopher to object to ag biotech on explicitly ethical grounds." I then wrote a series of other articles objecting to GM herbicide-resistant crops, transgenic animals, and, indeed, all of ag biotech. I am acquainted with worries about GM foods. But, for reasons that include the weakness of the intrinsic objections, I have changed my mind. The sympathetic feelings on which my anti-GMO worldview was based did not survive the stirring up of reasoning. . . .

Distinguishing Religion and Ethics

Religious traditions provide an answer to the question, "How, overall, should I live my life?" Secular ethical traditions provide an answer to the question, "What is the right thing to do?" When in a pluralistic society a particular religion's answers come into genuine conflict with the answers arrived at through secular ethical deliberation, we must ask how deep is the conflict. If the conflict is so deep that honoring the religion's views would entail dishonoring another religion's views, then we have a difficult decision to make. In such cases, the conclusions of secular ethical deliberation must override the answers of the religion in question.

The reason is that granting privileged status to one religion will inevitably discriminate against another religion. Individuals must be allowed to follow their conscience in matters theological. But if one religion is allowed to enforce its values on others in a way that restricts the others' ability to pursue their values, then individual religious freedom has not been protected.

When Ethics Overrides Religion

Moral theorists refer to this feature of nonreligious ethical deliberation as the *overridingness* of ethics. If a parent refuses a life-saving medical procedure for a minor child on religious grounds, the state is justified in overriding the parent's religious beliefs in order to protect what secular ethics regards as a value higher than religious freedom: the life of a child.

The overridingness of ethics applies to our discussion only if a religious group claims the right to halt GM technology on purely religious grounds. The problem here is the confessional problem of one group attempting to enforce its beliefs on others. I mean no disrespect to religion; as I have noted, I am a religious person, and I value religious traditions other than my own. Religious traditions have been the repositories and incubators of virtuous behavior. Yet each of our traditions must in a global society learn to coexist peacefully with competing religions and with nonreligious traditions and institutions.

If someone objects to GM technology on purely religious grounds, we must ask on what authority they speak for their tradition, whether there are other, conflicting, views within their tradition and whether acting on their views will entail disrespecting the views of people from other religions. It is, of course, the right of each tradition to decide its attitude about genetic engineering. But in the absence of other good reasons, we must not allow someone to ban GM technology for narrowly sectarian reasons alone. To allow such an action would be to disrespect the views of people who believe, on equally sincere religious grounds, that GM technology is not necessarily inconsistent with God's desires for us. . . .

I personally came to change my mind about the moral acceptability of GM crops. My opinion changed as I took full account of three considerations: (i) the rights of people in various countries to choose to adopt GM technology (a consideration falling under the human rights principle); (ii) the balance of likely benefits over harms to consumers and the environment from GM technology (a utilitarian consideration); and (iii) the wisdom of encouraging discovery, innovation, and careful regulation of GM technology (a consideration related to virtue theory).

Is it ethically justifiable to pursue GM crops and foods? I have come to believe that three of our most influential ethical traditions converge on a common answer. Assuming we proceed responsibly and with appropriate caution, the answer is yes.

Periodical Bibliography

The following articles have been selected to supplement the diverse views presented in this chapter.

Ronald Bailey — "Warning: Bioethics May Be Hazardous to Your Health," *Reason*, August/September 1999.

Harold W. Baillie — "Genetic Engineering and Our Human Nature," *Philosophy & Public Policy Quarterly*, Winter/Spring 2003.

Lawrence I. Bonchek — "Stem Cells, Embryos, and Casualties of War," *Free Inquiry*, Summer 2002.

Shelley Burtt — "Which Babies?: Dilemmas of Genetic Testing," *Tikkun*, January/February 2001.

Thomas W. Clark — "Playing God, Carefully," *Humanist*, May 2000.

Kevin Clarke — "Unnatural Selection," *U.S. Catholic*, January 2000.

Eric Cohen — "New Genetics, Old Quandries: Debating the Biotech Utopia," *Weekly Standard*, April 22, 2002.

Ronald Cole-Turner — "Genes and Genesis: Religion and Genetic Testing," *Park Ridge Center Bulletin*, January/February 2000.

Commonweal — "Of Mice, Jellyfish and Us," *Commonweal*, January 28, 2000.

Jacques Diouf — "Like 'An Axe in the Hands of a Pathological Criminal'?" *UN Chronicle*, September–November 2001.

David R. Gergen — "Trouble in Paradise," *U.S. News & World Report*, August 20, 2001.

Deal W. Hudson — "Stem Cells Equal Baby Parts," *Crisis*, May 2000.

William F. Jasper — "Latest Assault on the Preborn," *New American*, August 27, 2001.

Brewster Kneen — "Caring for Life: Genetic Engineering and Agriculture," *Ecumenical Review*, July 2002.

M. Therese Lysaught — "Let's Make the World a No-Clone Zone," *U.S. Catholic*, April 2003.

Gilbert Meilaender — "Spare Embryos: If They're Going to Die Anyway, Does That Really Entitle Us to Treat Them as Handy Research Material?" *Weekly Standard*, August 26–September 2, 2002.

James M. Pethokoukis, Simon Smith, and Eric Cohen	"Humanity 2.0," *U.S. News & World Report*, August 29, 2003.
John A. Robertson	"Ethics and Policy in Embryonic Stem Cell Research," *Kennedy Institute of Ethics Journal*, June 1999.
Thomas A. Shannon	"The Human Genome: Now the Hard Work and the Hard Questions," *Commonweal*, March 23, 2001.
Peter Singer	"Stem Cells and Immortal Souls," *Free Inquiry*, Spring 2000.
Wesley J. Smith	"Is Bioethics Ethical?" *Weekly Standard*, April 3, 2000.
Tracey Walker	"Fast Forward: Predicting the Future with Genetic Testing Requires Ethical Forethought," *Managed Healthcare Executive*, July 2003.
Rick Weiss	"Building a Better Baby: Embryo Screening Creates a Tool Against Disease but Raises Ethical Questions," *Washington Post*, July 9, 2001.

CHAPTER 3

What Is the Impact of Genetically Engineered Crops?

Chapter Preface

Genetically modified (GM) foods have been the source of heated debate, with GM corn often at the center of controversy. American corn farmers have faced a constant battle with the corn borer, a voracious insect that costs farmers nearly $1 billion a year in pesticides and other measures to prevent damage to corn crops. In 1995 scientists from Plant Genetics Systems developed corn seed it called StarLink, which contained a corn borer–killing gene that poisoned the borer, saving farmers time and money. Because StarLink contained a protein, Cry9C, that resembled a substance found to trigger violent allergies in some people, U.S. federal regulators threatened to ban it. Aventis, a European pharmaceutical company that had purchased Plant Genetic Systems, asked if it could instead sell the StarLink seed to farmers who would use it only for feed corn and who would in turn promise not to sell it to anyone who might put it in human food. The Environmental Protection Agency (EPA) agreed. StarLink comprised only .5 percent of the 80 million acres of corn planted in the United States at that time, yet in September 2000 StarLink began to show up in food, including tacos, corn chips, and muffin mix.

Once the release of StarLink into the human food supply had been officially confirmed, Aventis immediately accepted responsibility. Some commentators claim, however, that the blame should have been shared. According to business journalist Brian O'Reilly, "The promises made by StarLink's inventors proved worthless, falling prey to managerial inattention, corporate mergers, blind faith, misplaced hope, woeful ignorance, political activism, and probably greedy farmers too." Nevertheless, the brunt of the blame was assigned to and accepted by Aventis, and the company immediately suspended sale of the seeds. Moreover, although the corporation never agreed with assertions made about the allergic effects of StarLink, it acted immediately to mitigate the alleged damage, ultimately spending well over $100 million. O'Reilly maintains, "To its belated credit, Aventis has been aggressively trying to locate StarLink seed. . . . The company has also paid for millions of test kits used by farmers, food processors, and grain handlers to identify traces of StarLink."

Other observers place the blame on opponents of GM foods, who took advantage of the situation to generate fear in the American consumer. On September 18, 2000, a coalition of health, consumer, and environmental groups calling themselves Genetically Engineered Food Alert made national headlines with the announcement that Kraft taco shells marketed under the Taco Bell name tested positive for StarLink. After the announcement, thirty-seven people reported allergic reactions. Initial studies by the EPA, the Food and Drug Administration (FDA), and the Centers for Disease Control (CDC) indicated that seven of these cases might have been linked to StarLink, but in June 2001 the CDC found no evidence that StarLink corn caused allergic reactions in those who consumed it. Despite the CDC report, a federal scientific advisory panel conducted public hearings and concluded that Cry9C appeared enough like its allergen cousin to prohibit its use in human food. For health writer Jim Thornton, the StarLink story revealed the effectiveness of scare tactics:

> Reporters could easily spin this as a story in which farmers and consumers are victims and the villains are the reckless Dr. Frankensteins of the biotech firms—aided and abetted by lax EPA regulators. But it's worth pausing to remember that no one was actually shown to be injured by Star Link. The lawsuits that occurred at the time—from a handful of customers concerned that they might be having allergic reactions to the corn—and the subsequent financial losses suffered by the farmers were all fear-driven, not the result of good science showing that stomach upset was any more likely among (non-frightened, non-litigious) StarLink eaters than among ordinary taco shell eaters.

The StarLink scare was short lived and had little impact on American consumption of GM foods. In fact, in 2003 U.S. GM corn plantings increased 40 percent from the previous year as farmers sowed 31.6 million acres of GM corn varieties. Nevertheless, commentators continue to debate whether StarLink corn was actually harmful. In the following chapter authors debate the impact of genetically engineered crops such as StarLink corn.

"The risks of genetically engineered foods vastly outweigh any benefits."

Genetically Engineered Crops Are Dangerous

John Grogan and Cheryl Long

Consumers should be concerned about the dangers of genetically engineered crops because the outcome of genetic changes is unpredictable, claim John Grogan and Cheryl Long in the following viewpoint. When crops are engineered to tolerate weed killers and pesticides, the authors claim, other characteristics of the plant may also change, causing allergic reactions in consumers. Moreover, the authors maintain, corporations that have patented these crops and therefore own them are motivated by profit, not public safety. Grogan and Long are on the editorial staff of *Organic Gardening*.

As you read, consider the following questions:
1. According to the authors, what percentage of U.S. cropland is covered by genetically engineered crops?
2. In the authors' opinion, why could some organic farmers lose their certification?
3. How does traditional farmers' relationship to nature differ from those who follow the genetic engineering agricultural model, in the authors' view?

John Grogan and Cheryl Long, "The Problem with Genetic Engineering," *Organic Gardening*, vol. 47, January 2000, pp. 42–47. Copyright © 2000 by Rodale Press. Reproduced by permission.

A new millennium is dawning, and with it a new age. For the first time, humans are able to manipulate the very fabric of life, shuffling the genetic deck that controls every aspect of every living organism in ways that nature never intended. It began in 1971 with a microscopic bacterium that was genetically altered to devour oil spills. Today, a powerful, profit-driven industry, comprised largely of the same companies that have made their fortunes in chemical pesticides, has sprung up around this new science. Genetically engineered crops cover an estimated one-quarter of all cropland in the United States: about half of all the soybeans and cotton grown, and a third of all corn.

This science of tinkering with nature in the hope of improving upon it is a heady business. By splicing genes and dicing DNA, scientists may someday cure dreaded diseases and create powerful vaccines. But what offers such promise in the tightly controlled laboratories of medicine raises deeply troubling implications in the open fields and yards of the world's farms and gardens. With regard to genetically altered life-forms, once a mistake is made and released into the environment, there is no certainty it can ever be undone.

Here at *Organic Gardening*, we know such a highly unnatural technology would never have a place in our definition of organic gardening, but we have resisted a rush to judgment. Monsanto, DuPont, and other major corporate players in the emerging genetic engineering market have argued that their products hold the power to feed the world while cutting pesticide use and curbing erosion.

Yet the more information we gather, studies we read, and scientific debates we monitor, the more convinced we become that those claims are overblown at best and that the science of biotechnology is lurching forward far too rapidly and with neither adequate study nor precaution. The lack of rigorous, independent study and government regulation heightens our concern.

A Chorus of Critics

A rising chorus of scientists, academics, and ethicists is voicing alarm at this exploding, and largely uncharted, technology. Jane Rissler, Ph.D., a former biotechnology regulator with the Environmental Protection Agency (EPA) who is now with the Union of Concerned Scientists, says, "We're skeptical of the benefits of this technology, and we're concerned about the risks. We think there are better alternatives to solving challenges in agriculture, and the public should have a say in how the technology is used and developed."

The public's say is critical. Consumers have no way to know when they are eating genetically altered foods. That's because the Food and Drug Administration [FDA] has chosen not to classify alien genes as food additives and therefore does not require that they be listed on food labels. A bag of corn chips, for instance, must disclose that salt has been added, but it need not reveal that the corn itself has been genetically manipulated to contain its own pesticide. At a minimum, shouldn't shoppers have a right to make informed decisions?

"Labeling is the first step, because it gives people the right to choose," says Richard Wolfson, Ph.D., the Canadian chairman of the Consumer Right to Know Campaign, an umbrella organization for numerous groups that are calling for mandatory labeling and long-term testing of all genetically engineered foods. "Without labeling, there's no way to trace any health effects, and there is no way to protect consumers."

A Growing Demand for Labeling

Around the world, protests continue to mount against these genetically modified "Frankenfoods," as they have been dubbed. The European Union has banned virtually all genetically altered corn imports, effectively freezing out all U.S. corn until recently because modified varieties were not separated from the rest of the crop. The cost to American farmers was about $200 million in 1998. Japan is demanding labeling of genetically engineered foods. Americans have been far more willing to accept such foods without question, but that is now changing. Two lawsuits demanding labeling have been filed against the FDA[1] and [in 1999] Congress received half a

1. On May 27, 1998, a coalition of public interest groups, scientists, and religious leaders filed a lawsuit against the FDA to obtain mandatory safety testing and labeling of all genetically engineered (GE) foods. On September 29, 2000, a federal judge dismissed the suit. On February 18, 1999, an international coalition of public interest organizations filed a lawsuit in federal court to have all Bt (Bacillus

million signatures on petitions calling for labeling of gene-altered foods. Several other campaigns are now under way. . . .

In addition to not requiring labeling of these foods, the FDA does not demand testing of them. It requires only the manufacturer's assurance that they are safe. Similarly, the U.S. Department of Agriculture and the EPA have no comprehensive testing requirements.

"There is no meaningful, scientifically credible process across all federal government agencies to evaluate the hazards of genetically engineered organisms," says Suzanne Wuerthele, Ph.D., an EPA risk-assessment expert. "The bottom line, in my personal view, is that we are confronted with the most powerful technology the world has ever known, and it is being rapidly deployed with almost no thought whatsoever to its consequences."

Here are 10 reasons why all of us should be troubled about the rapid proliferation of genetically engineered foods.

The Superbugs and Superweeds

[1] Superbugs: Of the 50 or so genetically engineered plants currently cleared by the government for use, most fall into two basic categories: plants engineered to include their own pesticide, a toxin produced by the BT *(Bacillus thuringiensis)* bacterium, and plants engineered to survive weed killers, including the so-called Roundup Ready soybeans and cotton.

BT is a natural and highly effective pesticide that has long been used by organic growers to control caterpillars and other pests. But what organic farmers and gardeners use sparingly, biotechnology has introduced into each cell of every genetically engineered plant, from the roots to the pollen to the chaff plowed under after harvest. Because of BT's ubiquitous presence in millions of acres of crops, even the industry's own scientists concede that it is just a matter of time—as little as 3 to 5 years—before BT-resistant insect strains evolve. Directives that farmers interplant these BT-carrying crops with non-modified varieties is expected to merely delay the inevitable.

thuringiensis) crops taken off of the market on the grounds that they are not properly labeled and that lack of mandatory labeling illegally restricts the freedom of choice to avoid GE foods. The suit was dismissed on July 26, 2000.

And when the inevitable happens, organic growers will lose a powerful pest control, and conventional growers will return to chemical pesticides—unless, of course, biotechnology can come up with yet a new generation of pest-immune crops.

Besides, although there is no evidence that BT-carrying crops hurt humans, there is something unsettling about eating food that is itself a pesticide registered with the EPA. Unlike conventional pesticides, the built-in BT bug killer cannot be washed off; it is in every bite.

[2] Superweeds: Scientists also warn that some herbicide-tolerant crops are cross-pollinating with wild cousins and could create herbicide-resistant weeds. Another threat, according to Dr. Rissler, is that some genetically engineered crops themselves, bred to resist insects and other natural controls, could become invasive, spreading beyond their fields and choking out natural habitats.

Unexpected Effects

[3] Pollen drift: Organic farmers could lose their certification and face huge financial losses if their fields are contaminated by wind-borne pollen from neighboring genetically modified crops. Even nonorganic farmers are at risk for problems. In Canada, Monsanto accused canola grower Percy Schmeiser of patent infringement after the company allegedly found genetically engineered Roundup Ready canola plants in Schmeiser's fields. Schmeiser claims he never planted any Monsanto seeds. After mediation efforts failed, he filed a $10 million lawsuit against Monsanto, claiming libel, trespass, and contamination of his fields.[2]

[4] Harm to wildlife: Cornell University researchers made headlines when they announced laboratory research showing that monarch butterfly larvae died after eating milkweed dusted with genetically engineered corn pollen containing the BT pesticide. Milkweed, the monarch's primary food source, commonly grows alongside corn. Researchers in Eu-

2. The Federal Court of Canada issued their judgment in the case of *Monsanto vs. Schmeiser Enterprises* on March 29, 2001, finding Percy Schmeiser violated Monsanto Canada Inc.'s patent on Roundup Ready canola technology. The ruling was upheld on appeal. On May 8, 2003, the Supreme Court of Canada granted Schmeiser's application for Leave to Appeal. As of this writing, it has not reached a decision.

ALL I DID WAS SQUEEZE A TOMATO TO DETERMINE HOW FIRM IT WAS...

GENETICALLY ALTERED VEGETABLES

Cam. © 2003 by Cagle Cartoons. Reproduced by permission.

rope have made similar discoveries involving ladybugs and green lacewings, both beneficial insects. Yet another study, reported in 1997 in the British publication *New Scientist*, indicates that honeybees may be harmed by feeding on proteins found in genetically engineered canola flowers.

[5] Harm to soil: Microbiologists at New York University have found that the BT toxin in residues of genetically altered corn and rice crops persists in soils for up to 8 months and depresses microbial activity. And in another study, scientists in Oregon tested an experimental genetically engineered soil microbe in the laboratory and found it *killed* wheat plants when it was added to the soil in which they were grown.

The Impact on Humans

[6] Human health: Even as the biotech industry and government regulators have assured us that there is no reason to worry, a growing body of evidence indicates that genetic engineering can cause unintended changes to our food, making it less nutritious or even harmful. For example, a study in a 1998–99 issue of the *Journal of Medicinal Food* indicates that compared with nonmodified soy varieties, genetically altered,

herbicide-tolerant varieties may contain lower levels of potentially beneficial plant estrogens. Another study, reported in a 1996 article in the *International Journal of Health Services*, warns that milk produced from cows injected with Monsanto's controversial genetically engineered bovine growth hormone (BGH) contains higher levels of a growth factor that may be linked to increased risk of both breast and gastrointestinal cancers in humans. Americans have been drinking unlabeled BGH-produced milk for years, but it has always been banned in Canada and Europe.

[7] Hidden allergens: The foundation of genetic engineering is DNA, which directs the production of proteins. Proteins are also common sources of human allergies. When DNA from one organism is spliced into another, then, can it turn a nonallergenic food into one that will cause an allergic reaction in some people? Yes, reported researchers in *The New England Journal of Medicine* (NEJM) in 1996. The case involved an attempt by the Iowa-based biotech seed company Pioneer Hi-Bred International to change the protein content of soybeans by adding a gene from the Brazil nut. When researchers tested the modified soybean on people with sensitivity to Brazil nuts (but no sensitivity to soybeans), they found it triggered an allergic reaction. Based on those findings, the company shelved development of the soybean. But, wrote the author of an editorial in the same NEJM issue, "the next case could be less ideal, and the public less fortunate."

[8] Religious and moral considerations: People who choose not to eat animals for religious or moral reasons face an almost impossible task with many genetically engineered foods. When cold-hardiness genes from flounder are spliced into tomatoes, or genes from chickens are added to potatoes for increased disease resistance, are those vegetables still, purely speaking, *vegetables*? And without mandatory labeling, how can people who object to eating any trace of meat know what they are getting?

[9] Antibiotic resistance: Genetic engineers use antibiotic *marker genes* to help them transfer genetic coding from one life-form to another. But some scientists worry that this process could compound the already serious problem of antibi-

otic resistance in humans. Government scientists in Britain warn that the antibiotic resistance introduced into humans from genetically modified foods could render established medical treatments for such infections as meningitis and gonorrhea ineffective.

[10] Indentured farmers: Because genetic engineering research is so expensive, it is largely controlled by for-profit corporations whose primary goal is return on investment, not public good. These corporations are rapidly buying up seed companies and gaining control of entire food-production systems and educational-research facilities. Farmers who use this patented technology, meanwhile, are prohibited from the time-honored tradition of saving seed to use the following season. They are forced into a costly cycle of corporate dependency.

The Threat of "Progress"

For these and other reasons, we at *Organic Gardening* believe the risks of genetically engineered foods vastly outweigh any benefits. Biotechnology may indeed prove to be to the twenty-first century what the steam engine was to the nineteenth century and what the computer was to the twentieth. But nothing inherent in this technology assures that the changes will be good. The biggest concern is not what society knows about genetic manipulation but what it does not know. History, from DDT to Love Canal, has been strewn with the inadvertent consequences of "progress." It would be the height of hubris to assume that tinkering with evolution, in all its complexity, could have no unforeseen fallout.

The results of 50 years of chemical-based "high-tech" agriculture have made clear that we must rethink the way we grow food. The answer, we believe, lies in a return to sustainable, organic growing practices. Biotechnology is merely the next rung on the chemical-farming ladder, providing yet another artificial tool to help perpetuate the shortsighted and unsustainable practices of monoculture agriculture. Monsanto says its herbicide-tolerant crops reduce the need for tilling, preventing erosion. But smart organic practices—employing cover crops, mulches, and other natural techniques—control erosion just as efficiently without the use of dangerous chemicals, and they create healthy soil in the process.

Traditionally, farmers have had the closest connection to the natural world, and the deepest understanding of human dependency on the diversity of wild plants and animals. Yet genetic engineering, like the generation of chemical-based solutions before it, perpetuates an agricultural model far removed from nature.

Today, the conventional farmer sits upon a giant tractor, inside an air-conditioned cab, moving through huge fields of a single crop. If the birds stop singing, will he hear the silence? If the monarch butterflies stop fluttering over the milkweed in the fencerow, will he even notice?

Our children and grandchildren have just one future. Are we willing to risk it?

"Three federal agencies share responsibility for ensuring . . . that foods and crops developed through biotechnology are at least as safe as their 'conventional' counterparts."

Genetically Engineered Crops Are Not Dangerous

L. Val Giddings

In the following viewpoint L. Val Giddings argues that genetically engineered crops are safe for people and the environment. Allegations against genetically engineered crops are based on myths and misrepresentations, he maintains. Opponents argue that these crops are inadequately regulated, but Giddings contends that before a genetically engineered crop can be planted, three federal agencies must find that they are as safe a conventionally bred crop. Moreover, claims Giddings, genetically engineered crops can make the world a greener, healthier place. Giddings is vice president for food and agriculture at the Biotechnology Industry Organization.

As you read, consider the following questions:
1. In the author's opinion, how long is the average research, development, and regulatory process for a typical genetically engineered crop?
2. According to Giddings, how long have humans been engaged in genetic modification?
3. How many questions will the biotechnology industry have to answer to satisfy its critics, in the author's view?

B ased on the overwhelming body of scientific evidence supporting the safety of bioengineered crops, the answer [to the question should consumers be concerned about bio-engineered crops] is resoundingly "no." James Watson, Nobel Prize–winning biologist and codiscoverer of the DNA double helix, said it best years ago: "When considering the risks of re-combinant DNA, we shy at kittens and cuddle tigers."

Critics of agricultural biotechnology harp on a series of myths and misstatements to support their position that these foods and crops are unsafe. Let's examine the most prevalent.

Minding the Store

The first myth is that we should be fearful and cautious— even to the point of moratoriums or bans—of innovations brought to agriculture through biotechnology because "no one is minding the shop." According to this thesis, compa-nies haphazardly develop and commercialize what they want with inadequate regard for consumer safety or the environ-ment. Not true. Crops and foods improved through bio-technology have been subjected to more scrutiny—in ad-vance, and in more depth and detail—than any foods in history. An open and abundant record documenting this scrutiny is available to anyone who is curious.

Three federal agencies share responsibility for ensuring, in advance, that foods and crops developed through biotech-nology are at least as safe as their "conventional" counter-parts. The U.S. Department of Agriculture (USDA), the Environmental Protection Agency (EPA) and the Food and Drug Administration (FDA) oversee crops and foods ac-cording to a road map laid out in 1986—known as the "Co-ordinated Framework."

According to this framework, the USDA handles any po-tential threats to U.S. agriculture and the environment, the FDA safeguards the food supply, and the EPA deals both with crops improved to resist insects and with environmen-tal issues not covered elsewhere.

In the course of this regulatory oversight, the typical crop developed through biotechnology travels a research, develop-ment and regulatory pathway that takes, on average, 12 years and generates volumes of analytical and safety studies. During this process, every reasonable question related to food safety imaginable is asked and answered. If any of the answers reveals material differences between the biotech and conventional crop or food, the differences guide the further examination required before a finding of safety can be reached.

The first biotechnology-enhanced whole food—the Flavr Savr tomato produced by Calgene in 1992—generated enough regulatory-review documents to occupy 6 feet of shelf space. Compare this with the regulatory oversight visited upon a tomato produced through conventional breeding. The contrast is telling.

The Biotech Farmer

Another myth is that farmers adopt the technology only because they have no choice and are backing away from it in the face of customer rejection. The facts again tell a different story: USDA statistics show that for the 2001 growing season, the proportion of U.S. acreage devoted to crops improved through biotechnology continues to increase. It currently stands at 68 percent for soybeans (up from 54 percent last year), 69 percent for cotton (up from 61 percent) and 26 percent for corn.

Recent reports from an independent agricultural analyst confirm the benefits biotechnology has brought, is bringing and can bring not only to these major-commodity crops, but also to other crops, including some in desperate need of help. Family farmers are not fools. They carefully weigh and evaluate their planting choices and hedge their bets. Their strong, rapid embrace of biotechnology provides eloquent testimony to the benefits of these crops.

The Label Lobby

There are a host of other myths. Critics claim, for example, that the industry is opposed to labeling foods because it has something to hide, that biotech corn kills monarch butterflies and that the StarLink-corn episode shows biotech crops are unsafe and cannot be controlled.

Let's begin with food labels. Who possibly could be opposed to providing consumers with information labels relating to health, safety and nutrition? The answer is, of course, nobody. But advocates of labeling for biotech foods are not calling for labels that tell information about health, safety and nutrition that is accurate and informative. Such labels are required by law, have been supported by the biotech industry, and have included foods improved through biotech since 1992.

Big Rise in U.S. Biotech Crops

U.S. farmers have adopted genetically modified crop varieties at a rapid rate since their introduction in 1996, driven by expectations of lower production costs, higher yields and reduced pesticide use. Herbicide-tolerant (HT) soybeans, for example, expanded from about 17 percent of soybean acreage in 1997 to more than 50 percent in 2000.

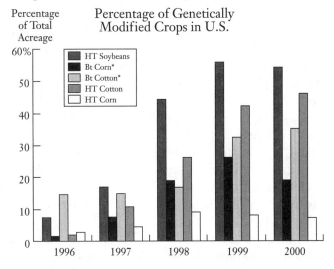

Percentage of Total Acreage

Percentage of Genetically Modified Crops in U.S.

Legend:
- HT Soybeans
- Bt Corn*
- Bt Cotton*
- HT Cotton
- HT Corn

*Bt crops contain *Bacillus thuringiengis*, a naturally occurring soil bacteria that kills insects.

Economic Research Service; U.S. Department of Agriculture, 2001.

Those clamoring for special labels simply want to stigmatize foods improved through biotech, while they misrepresent the rigorous regulatory process and proven safety of these products. Such labels will allow them to organize boycotts and economic blackmail.

They argue that special labels are required to ensure "consumer choice" for those who want to stick to "natural" foods.

Never mind that 10 millennia of artificial selection by humans means that virtually nothing on a dinner plate in the industrial world would be recognized by our hunter-gatherer ancestors of not so long ago. Those ancestors would marvel at the blessings crude genetic modification have brought to humanity through improved crops and livestock.

"Natural" corn has an ear the size of the last digit of your little finger. "Natural" tomatoes are the size of a grape, and a stunted one at that. "Natural" wheat appears to be a cross between at least three grass species. And poodles are nothing less than genetically modified wolves. Products of modern biotechnology, by contrast, result from manipulations with specific intent from the greatest base of human knowledge and understanding in history, with the greatest degree of precision and predictability—and therefore safety assurance—that we have ever had.

The Monarch Butterfly Myth

Another myth: monarch butterflies. One quick-and-dirty lab experiment resulted in numerous stories about threats to "the 'Bambi' of the insect world," indeed to all biodiversity, from toxic clouds of biotech corn pollen. The dramatic images again are contradicted by reality.

But here is the crux—even if biotech corn pollen killed monarchs outside the laboratory and in the field (for which there still is no evidence), the question should be: Does it kill more or less than the alternative? Of the nearly dozen available corn varieties containing *Bt* (a naturally occurring soil bacteria that acts as an insecticide), only one (now retired at the natural end of its commercial life) had the potential to be toxic to exposed monarch larvae. That one variety was never grown on more than 2 percent of the U.S. corn acreage. And even then, it was in places where the potential was extremely low for corn pollen occurring while monarch larvae were present.

If the alternative to *Bt* corn is pesticide sprays, there's no contest. Insecticide sprays are nonselective, killing almost all insects—adults and feeding larvae—whenever applied. *Bt* corn pollen, at worst, would be a problem for only a small portion of the monarch larvae present throughout the breeding season and only in limited areas.

Two years of field research confirmed that not only were the risk assessments preceding introduction of *Bt* corn correct in concluding minimal risk to monarchs but that, because of various factors a *Bt* cornfield actually might be the safest place for a monarch to lay its eggs! Another myth debunked.

A Harmless Mistake

And finally, StarLink. Here is a genuine black eye for the industry. There is no getting around it. The fact that a variety of corn not approved for human use entered the human food supply may be understandable, but it was inexcusable. But let us keep the matter in perspective.

Even after StarLink, the reality is this: Although humans around the world during the last decade have eaten hundreds of millions of tons of foods derived from crops improved through biotechnology, there still is not so much as a single, solitary sniffle or headache positively linked to their consumption. This safety record is the envy of conventional- and organic-food production.

StarLink represents a rare failure of the regulatory system, not a threat to human health. It is a failure the industry united to pledge would not be repeated, even before the federal regulatory agencies moved to close the regulatory gate through which it had slipped—the possibility of "split approvals" (i.e., approval for animal feed but not human food use) for major-commodity crops. It never should have happened, and it will not happen again.

The recent report by the FDA and the Centers for Disease Control and Prevention that individuals claiming allergic reactions to eating foods containing corn had no antibodies to the StarLink protein further reinforces the argument that even had it been an allergen, the exposure level was too low to result in allergic reactions.

Many other myths collide fatally with reality once rhetoric is set aside and the facts are considered dispassionately. The question then arises, "How many questions have to be answered before the critics will withdraw their objections to biotechnology in agriculture?"

The answer now is apparent: For some, no answers are sufficient because the questions are only a means to an end.

The end is opposition to what is seen as increasing concentration and corporate control of agriculture. I would respond with a simple thought experiment—wave a magic wand and make biotechnology go away. How many of the problems of concentration and economic transformation in agriculture vanish with biotechnology? None.

Biotechnology is, at least in part, a solution to many problems. But it is inarguable that the companies applying biotechnology to agriculture are leaving untouched many opportunities, especially those that would benefit the poorest of the poor. A constructive resolution might be had: If more of us joined in a rational, fact-based debate about biotechnology and got behind increased public-sector support for biotechnology (and all effective appropriate technologies) aimed at areas corporate research is unlikely to cover, the possibilities for progress would improve substantially. In the end, we could leave our children a much greener, richer, healthier world than we found. Why not do it?

"Genetic engineering may be the most
environmentally beneficial technology to
have emerged in decades, or possibly
centuries."

Genetically Engineered Crops
Protect the Environment

Jonathan Rauch

Genetically engineered crops can protect the earth from the
damage caused by farming techniques such as ploughing and
irrigation, argues Jonathan Rauch in the following viewpoint. Some genetically engineered crops are resistant to
weed killers, he contends, allowing farmers to kill weeds
without ploughing, and others are salt tolerant, which means
they can be planted in land that has high salinity as a result
of irrigation. Returning abused farmland to productivity using genetically engineered crops makes unnecessary the con-
version of wild habitat into cropland, he maintains. Rauch is
a writer in residence at the Brookings Institution in Washington, D.C.

As you read, consider the following questions:

1. According to Rauch, what are some of the trade-offs of
   organic, traditional, and low-input farming techniques?
2. What do many "greens" call organisms resulting from
   gene transfers, according to Rauch?
3. In Dennis Avery's opinion, what would have happened if
   farming techniques had not improved since 1950?

Jonathan Rauch, "Will Frankenfood Save the Planet?" *Atlantic Monthly*, vol. 292,
October 2003, pp. 103–108.

That genetic engineering may be the most environmentally beneficial technology to have emerged in decades, or possibly centuries, is not immediately obvious. Certainly, at least, it is not obvious to the many U.S. and foreign environmental groups that regard biotechnology as a bête noire. Nor is it necessarily obvious to people who grew up in cities, and who have only an inkling of what happens on a modern farm. . . .

The Environmental Stress of Farming

It is only a modest exaggeration to say that as goes agriculture, so goes the planet. Of all the human activities that shape the environment, agriculture is the single most important, and it is well ahead of whatever comes second. Today about 38 percent of the earth's land area is cropland or pasture—a total that has crept upward over the past few decades as global population has grown. The increase has been gradual, only about 0.3 percent a year; but that still translates into an additional Greece or Nicaragua cultivated or grazed every year.

Farming does not go easy on the earth, and never has. To farm is to make war upon millions of plants (weeds, so–called) and animals (pests, so-called) that in the ordinary course of things would crowd out or eat or infest whatever it is a farmer is growing. Crop monocultures, as whole fields of only wheat or corn or any other single plant are called, make poor habitat and are vulnerable to disease and disaster. Although fertilizer runs off and pollutes water, farming without fertilizer will deplete and eventually exhaust the soil. Pesticides can harm the health of human beings and kill desirable or harmless bugs along with pests. Irrigation leaves behind trace elements that can accumulate and poison the soil. And on and on.

The trade-offs are fundamental. Organic farming, for example, uses no artificial fertilizer, but it does use a lot of manure, which can pollute water and contaminate food. Traditional farmers may use less herbicide, but they also do more ploughing, with all the ensuing environmental complications. Low-input agriculture uses fewer chemicals but more land. The point is not that farming is an environmental crime—it is not—but that there is no escaping the pressure it puts on the planet.

Feeding the Growing Population

In the next half century the pressure will intensify. The United Nations, in its midrange projections, estimates that the earth's human population will grow by more than 40 percent, from 6.3 billion people today to 8.9 billion in 2050. Feeding all those people, and feeding their billion or so hungry pets (a dog or a cat is one of the first things people want once they move beyond a subsistence lifestyle), and providing the increasingly protein-rich diets that an increasingly wealthy world will expect—doing all of that will require food output to at least double, and possibly triple.

But then the story will change. According to the UN's midrange projections (which may, if anything, err somewhat on the high side), around 2050 the world's population will more or less level off. Even if the growth does not stop, it will slow. The crunch will be over. In fact, if in 2050 crop yields are still increasing, if most of the world is economically developed, and if population pressures are declining or even reversing—all of which seems reasonably likely—then the human species may at long last be able to feed itself, year in and year out, without putting any additional net stress on the environment. We might even be able to grow everything we need while *reducing* our agricultural footprint: returning cropland to wilderness, repairing damaged soils, restoring ecosystems, and so on. In other words, human agriculture might be placed on a sustainable footing forever: a breathtaking prospect.

The Role of Biotech

The great problem, then, is to get through the next four or five decades with as little environmental damage as possible. That is where biotechnology comes in. . . .

"Biotech" can refer to a number of things, but the relevant application here is genetic modification: the selective transfer of genes from one organism to another. Ordinary breeding can cross related varieties, but it cannot take a gene from a bacterium, for instance, and transfer it to a wheat plant. The organisms resulting from gene transfers are called "transgenic" by scientists—and "Frankenfood" by many greens [environmentalists].

Gene transfer poses risks, unquestionably. So, for that matter, does traditional crossbreeding. But many people worry that transgenic organisms might prove more unpredictable. One possibility is that transgenic crops would spread from fields into forests or other wild lands and there become environmental nuisances, or worse. A further risk is that transgenic plants might cross-pollinate with neighboring wild plants, producing "superweeds" or other invasive or destructive varieties in the wild. Those risks are real enough that even most biotech enthusiasts—including Dennis Avery [director of global food issues at the Hudson Institute], for example—favor some government regulation of transgenic crops.

Doing More Good than Harm

What is much less widely appreciated is biotech's potential to do the environment good. Take as an example continuous no-till farming which really works best with the help of transgenic crops. Human beings have been ploughing for so long that we tend to forget why we started doing it in the first place. The short answer: weed control. Turning over the soil between plantings smothers weeds and their seeds. If you don't plough, your land becomes a weed garden—unless you use herbicides to kill the weeds. Herbicides, however, are expensive and can be complicated to apply. And they tend to kill the good with the bad.

In the mid-1990s the agricultural-products company Monsanto introduced a transgenic soybean variety called Roundup Ready. As the name implies, these soybeans tolerate Roundup, an herbicide (also made by Monsanto) that kills many kinds of weeds and then quickly breaks down into harmless ingredients. Equipped with Roundup Ready crops, farmers found that they could retire their ploughs and control weeds with just a few applications of a single, relatively benign herbicide—instead of many applications of a complex and expensive menu of chemicals. More than a third of all U.S. soybeans are now grown without ploughing, mostly owing to the introduction of Roundup Ready varieties. Plough-less cotton farming has likewise received a big boost from the advent of bioengineered varieties. No-till farming without biotech is possible, but it's more difficult and expensive, which is why no-till and biotech are advancing in tandem.

Creating Tolerant Crops

In 2001 a group of scientists announced that they had engineered a transgenic tomato plant able to thrive on salty water—water, in fact, almost half as salty as seawater, and fifty times as salty as tomatoes can ordinarily abide. One of the researchers was quoted as saying, "I've already transformed tomato, tobacco, and canola. I believe I can transform any crop with this gene"—just the sort of Frankenstein hubris that makes environmentalists shudder. But consider the environmental implications. Irrigation has for millennia been a cornerstone of agriculture, but it comes at a price. As irrigation water evaporates, it leaves behind traces of salt, which accumulate in the soil and gradually render it infertile. (As any Roman legion knows, to destroy a nation's agricultural base you salt the soil.) Every year the world loses about 25 million acres—an area equivalent to a fifth of California—to salinity; 40 percent of the world's irrigated land, and 25 percent of America's, has been hurt to some degree. For decades traditional plant breeders tried to create salt-tolerant crop plants, and for decades they failed.

Salt-tolerant crops might bring millions of acres of wounded or crippled land back into production. "And it gets better," [plant physiologist] Alex Avery told me. The transgenic tomato plants take up and sequester in their leaves as much as six or seven percent of their weight in sodium. "Theoretically," Alex said, "you could reclaim a salt-contaminated field by growing enough of these crops to remove the salts from the soil."

His father [Dennis] chimed in: "We've worried about being able to keep these salt-contaminated fields going even for decades. We can now think about *centuries*."

The Biotech Crops

One of the first biotech crops to reach the market, in the mid-1990s, was a cotton plant that makes its own pesticide.

Scientists incorporated into the plant a toxin-producing gene from a soil bacterium known as *Bacillus thuringiensis*. With Bt cotton, as it is called, farmers can spray much less, and the poison contained in the plant is delivered only to bugs that actually eat the crop. As any environmentalist can tell you, insecticide is not very nice stuff—especially if you breathe it, which many Third World farmers do as they walk through their fields with backpack sprayers.

Taking the Pressure Off of the Environment

Even under the best of conditions, food production for hundreds of millions of Americans—and billions more around the globe—can take a toll on the environment. Erosion can claim precious topsoil; farm chemicals sometimes reach streams, rivers and groundwater supplies; and livestock can deplete grazing lands. Wetlands and other sensitive habitats sometimes get plowed under for use as farmland. And in the world's tropical forests where an estimated 90 percent of the world's species exist, poor farmers clear trees in order to provide food and a living for their families.

By improving many aspects of modern agriculture, biotechnology can help alleviate many of these pressures on the land, both by preserving natural resources and by reducing environmental stresses.

International Food Information Council, March 2002.

Transgenic cotton reduced pesticide use by more than two million pounds in the United States from 1996 to 2000, and it has reduced pesticide sprayings in parts of China by more than half. Earlier [in 2003] the Environmental Protection Agency approved a genetically modified corn that resists a beetle larva known as rootworm. Because rootworm is American corn's most voracious enemy, this new variety has the potential to reduce annual pesticide use in America by more than 14 million pounds. It could reduce or eliminate the spraying of pesticide on 23 million acres of U.S. land.

All of that is the beginning, not the end. Bioengineers are also working, for instance, on crops that tolerate aluminum, another major contaminant of soil, especially in the tropics. Return an acre of farmland to productivity, or double yields on an already productive acre, and, other things being equal, you reduce by an acre the amount of virgin forest or savannah that will be stripped and cultivated. That may be the most important benefit of all.

The Borlaug Hypothesis

Of the many people I have interviewed in my twenty years as a journalist, Norman Borlaug must be the one who has saved the most lives. Today he is an unprepossessing eighty-nine-year-old man of middling height, with crystal-bright blue eyes and thinning white hair. He still loves to talk about plant breeding, the discipline that won him the 1970 Nobel Peace Prize: Borlaug led efforts to breed the staples of the Green Revolution. Yet the renowned plant breeder is quick to mention that he began his career, in the 1930s, in forestry, and that forest conservation has never been far from his thoughts. In the 1960s, while he was working to improve crop yields in India and Pakistan, he made a mental connection. He would create tables detailing acres under cultivation and average yields—and then, in another column, he would estimate how much land had been saved by higher farm productivity. Later, in the 1980s and 1990s, he and others began paying increased attention to what some agricultural economists now call the Borlaug hypothesis: that the Green Revolution has saved not only many human lives but, by improving the productivity of existing farmland, also millions of acres of tropical forest and other habitat—and so has saved countless animal lives.

From the 1960s through the 1980s, for example, Green Revolution advances saved more than 100 million acres of wild lands in India. More recently, higher yields in rice, coffee, vegetables, and other crops have reduced or in some cases stopped forest-clearing in Honduras, the Philippines, and elsewhere. Dennis Avery estimates that if farming techniques and yields had not improved since 1950, the world would have lost an additional 20 million or so square miles of wildlife habitat, most of it forest. About 16 million square miles of forest exists today. "What I'm saying," Avery said, in response to my puzzled expression, "is that we have saved every square mile of forest on the planet."

Saving Habitat

Habitat destruction remains a serious environmental problem; in some respects it is the most serious. The savannahs and tropical forests of Central and South America, Asia, and Africa by and large make poor farmland, but they are the earth's storehouses of biodiversity, and the forests are the earth's lungs. Since 1972 about 200,000 square miles of Amazon rain forest have been cleared for crops and pasture; from 1966 to 1994 all but three of the Central American countries cleared more forest than they left standing. Mexico is losing more than 4,000 square miles of forest a year to peasant farms; sub-Saharan Africa is losing more than 19,000.

That is why the great challenge of the next four or five decades is not to feed an additional three billion people (and their pets) but to do so without converting much of the world's prime habitat into second- or third-rate farmland. Now, most agronomists agree that some substantial yield improvements are still to be had from advances in conventional breeding, fertilizers, herbicides, and other Green Revolution standbys. But it seems pretty clear that biotechnology holds more promise—probably much more. Recall that world food output will need to at least double and possibly triple over the next several decades. Even if production could be increased that much using conventional technology, which is doubtful, the required amounts of pesticide and fertilizer and other polluting chemicals would be immense. If properly developed, disseminated, and used, genetically modified crops might well be the best hope the planet has got.

"At a time when our environment is already suffering extreme stress we should avoid risking fragile balance or compounding our problems with genetic engineering."

Genetically Engineered Crops May Harm the Environment

Ricarda Steinbrecher

Genetic engineering is not a precise science—engineered crops have unpredictable and undesirable side effects that may harm the environment and disrupt local ecosystems, claims Ricarda Steinbrecher in the following viewpoint. If scientists splice an insecticide gene into a particular plant, she contends for example, the resulting decline in the insect population that feeds on that plant adversely impacts the birds and other insects that rely on it for food. Steinbrecher asserts that upsetting the balance of nature, which is becoming increasingly fragile in response to the growing human population, by genetically engineering crops is unwise. Steinbrecher is a genetic scientist and a member of the British Society for Allergy, Environmental, and Nutritional Medicine.

As you read, consider the following questions:

1. According to Steinbrecher, what is wrong with the concept of substantial equivalence?
2. In the author's opinion, what must be done to prevent a particular gene from being passed on to wild or weedy relatives?
3. What happens when a gene that is outside a plant's own control is permanently switched on, in the author's view?

Ricarda Steinbrecher, "What Is Wrong with Nature?" *Resurgence*, May/June 1998, pp. 16–19. Copyright © 1998 by Resurgence, Ltd. Reproduced by permission.

If we are to believe the advertisements and the bold promises of the biotech industry, world hunger will soon be a problem of the past. There will be no further threat to the environment, wildlife or biodiversity through modern agriculture, which depends so heavily on chemicals.

Making Bold Promises

Genetic engineering is the way forward. The few mishaps here and there will soon be sorted out. The unpredictability of Nature will be brought under control. Through genetic engineering, food will be better and safer than it ever has been. Plants are already grown that are made to be tolerant to herbicides (weed-killers) or resistant to insects and other pests. Other plants are being developed for resistance to fungal attack or to viruses.

And isn't it a great advance to have fruits that will not rot nor bruise nor ripen before told to do so; to produce vaccines in bananas and high concentrations of Vitamin A in rice and in rape seed? We can even use crop plants as factories by manipulating their genes so that they produce inedible chemicals and proteins and fibers for industrial purposes. Giant salmon are now grown so fast you can almost watch. Over-sized bulls produce more lean meat than anyone could have dreamed of. What is wrong with envisioning future plants and animals as tailor-made commodities? It seems that the only constraints on the possibilities of biotechnology are the boundaries of our imagination.

Asking the Right Questions

Even if all of these dreams were actually achievable and safe, society would have to question the ethics, the political implications, the monopolies created, the patenting of life, the socioeconomic effects, the costs to the environment, the impact on the Third World and on biodiversity. Or we could simply ask, "What is wrong with food and nature, as we know it?" The question we must surely ask be, are these technologies really safe? What are the dangers of genetic engineering itself? What are the associated hazards and risks? Do genetic scientists actually know what they are doing?

Hemophilia is the result of a failure of the gene for the

bloodclotting protein (Factor VIII) to work properly. The obvious solution is to replace the defective gene with an intact one. But our skills in genetic engineering do not allow such a precise "cut and paste job" among tens of thousands of genes. The best we can do at present is to add a functional gene without removing the bad one. This creates new problems. Where to place the new gene? On which chromosome? At which location? Next to which other gene? Will the inserted gene interfere with the function or activity of another nearby gene? Will it perform as it is supposed to, no matter where it is placed? Is there actually such a thing as an independent gene? Or are genes and other DNA sequences highly interactive and interdependent? And how can we find out? We do not as yet have the skills to place the gene exactly next to gene A or B or C. All we can do is try to get the gene integrated just somewhere along the chromosomes and hope it will not end up in the middle of another gene or near any regulatory sequences and cause havoc or constant background irritation. The risks involved for the individual are often high and the benefits more a suggestion than a reality.

Unpredictable Side Effects

What is true for gene therapy in humans is equally true for genetic engineering in plants and animals. Experiments have shown that a gene is not an independent entity as was originally thought. For example, a gene for the color red was the subject of an experiment in Germany in 1990. The color gene was taken from maize and—together with a gene for antibiotic resistance—was transferred into white petunia flowers. All that was expected was a whole field of 20,000 red flowers; yet not only did the genetically engineered flowers turn red, but they also had more leaves and shoots, a higher resistance to fungi and lowered fertility, all of which were completely unrelated to the color gene or the antibiotic resistance gene.

The genetically modified salmon reared in Scotland is another example. It may be growing fast, but, amongst other side effects, it is also turning green. Unrelated multiple side effects of this kind are now termed pleiotropic effects. They are, by their very nature, completely unpredictable.

In these cases the pleiotropic effects were easy to identify, without molecular analysis. But what happens if the unrelated side-effects are not so obvious—if they only affect protein composition, hormonal expression, nutrient or antinutrient concentration, toxins and allergens? Who is going to check all possible side effects before a plant is released into the environment or placed on our dinner plates? There are no regulations or voluntary practices, which check for these kinds of alteration.

The Problem with Substantial Equivalence

Pleiotropic effects like these are being overlooked by using the concept of substantial equivalence. Now implemented by the European Union (EU), this concept was advocated by the Organization for Economic Co-operation and Development (OECD) in the early 1990s as the most practical approach to addressing safety questions about foods derived by modern biotechnology.

A crucial 1996 report by the United Nations' Food and Agriculture Organization and World Health Organization stated in its recommendations: "Substantial equivalence embodies the concept that if a new food or food component is found to be substantially equivalent to an existing food or food component, it can be treated in the same manner with respect to safety." The report further states that if there are "defined differences" (e.g. an added gene for herbicide resistance or production of insecticides), the safety assessment should only focus on those defined differences. In effect that means, "Don't look for any of the side-effects mentioned above, just focus on the single trait or protein that was altered. And if this trait or protein was taken from a plant or animal that was part of our food chain, well, then this substance is substantially equivalent and can be passed as safe."

This approach gives a green light to a flood of engineered food, for which no long-term-risk assessments have been performed, and even short-term risks are swept under a regulatory carpet.

In another experiment, a red petunia had its red gene multiplied and amplified. Instead of obtaining a deeper red color, some of the 30,000 flowers were white; some pink,

153

and about half were red. And to confuse the geneticist even more, some of the red flowers reverted to white over time. This was one more experiment, which taught us how little we know. It now appears that this so-called gene silencing occurs when the plant has more than one copy of the same gene, that almost in a form of panic or utter confusion the plant just overrides the controls and puts the genes on ice, not to be used any more.

The Instability of Gene Splicing

Besides pleiotropic effects and gene silencing, there is a third complication—stability. Experiments with genetically engineered rice and other plants that had been given an extra gene revealed that over a few generations plants had either more or fewer copies of the gene than the parental generation. Does this mean that plants can perform surgery on themselves and cut the genes out? Or multiply them up and stick them in any odd place? Does that mean that some locations are particularly bad to insert genes into?

There are plenty more examples which show that our understanding of genes and their intricate communication and maintenance system is only just beginning. Yet our ability to chop and splice and multiply strings of DNA, to isolate and sequence them, has led some scientists and corporations to believe that we are well equipped with knowledge and expertise. They believe the time is ripe to transform plants and animals into designed and tailormade commodities.

But who will pay the price? Genes don't just stay put— they might move within the plant; they will certainly move into other plants by the same means that plants have cross-bred for millennia. For example, rapeseed easily cross-pollinates with wild radish, resulting in healthy and competitive hybrid plants. DNA fragments and even whole genes can be taken up by fungi or bacteria.

There is growing acceptance even amongst proponents of this technology, that gene transfer is inevitable and thus part of the package. Therefore, it is crucial that, if we don't want a particular gene to be passed on to wild or weedy relatives, we should not use it in the first place. This particularly applies to genes for herbicide tolerance and genes that produce insecticides or other chemicals to defend the plant against "attackers" such as bacteria, fungi or viruses.

The Dangers of Engineered Plants

Plants engineered to tolerate weed-killers will ultimately lead to an ever-increasing use of that weed killer, either due to the spread of the gene or due to weeds developing their own immunity. For example, annual rye grass (Lolium rigidum) in Australia has developed resistance to Monsanto's weed-killer "RoundUp." For the consumer, herbicide tolerant plants pose other dangers. Plants frequently sprayed with a weed-killer retain the chemical and people will ingest the residues of this chemical as well as its metabolites. Furthermore, plants grown in the presence of weed-killers can suffer from stress and react by over- or under-producing certain proteins or substances. Herbicide-tolerant members of the bean family are known to produce higher levels of plant-estrogens (phyto-oestrogens) when grown in the presence of glyphosate, the active ingredient of Monsanto's Roundup. Excessive concentrations of these estrogens present a potentially severe risk to children, as these plant-estrogens mimic the role of hormones in the body of humans or other mammals eating them. Estrogens are the female sex hormones—hence plant-estrogens may cause severe dysfunction of the reproductive system, especially in boys.

Plants with built-in insecticide pose further problems. Insects are part of the ecosystem and their numbers are naturally controlled by the abundance or rarity of their food sources and by predators such as birds or specialized insects such as ladybirds. The interaction between plants and insects has been a process of co-evolution rather than of extermination. Over time, plants have developed multiple defenses, such as hairiness, thorniness or the production of substances, which are toxic to posts. Plants produce an estimated 10,000 different "pesticide endotoxins" (insecticides) and other natural defense substances. It is important to the plant to get the balance right. Too much defense and there won't be enough energy and substance to fulfill other vital tasks, such as building seeds or growing strong stems or producing nutrients.

For some time now it has been standard agricultural practice to produce uniform fields of a single crop in the interests of high yields and efficient planting and harvesting. This has presented a problem to farmers because it sends out a loud and clear "Let's rave . . . !" signal to insects that live on that particular crop. They turn up in their thousands for the feast and this is when insects become "pests." Bio-technologists believe they can solve this problem with genes for toxin production. By inserting and permanently switching on these genes, they get plants to produce vast amounts of toxins to fight their own war, so we can forget about spraying them with nasty chemicals.

Scrambling the Tree of Life

Genetic Engineering enables the tree of life to be scrambled for the first time. It allows genes to be transferred across species boundaries, from any living organism into any other— animals to humans, humans to bacteria, microbes to plants, and so on. This could never happen in nature or through traditional breeding, where sows deliver piglets and roses make rosebuds.

Genetically engineered crops help North American farmers to intensify their production methods. Herbicide tolerant crops are drenched with chemicals to kill weeds better, Bt [Bacillus thuringiensis] crops produce toxins that kill insects, and virus-resistant crops resist viral infections by containing pieces of the virus. Potential impacts on the environment, already indicated by research, include growth of superweeds, the killing of beneficial as well as pest species, and creation of new viral diseases.

Bob Phelps, *Habitat Australia*, June 1999.

Any gene which is permanently switched on and which is outside the plant's own regulatory control can weaken the plant seriously. If a plant can't stop the production of a substance it does not commonly need for survival, it is prone to suffer system breakdown under prolonged stress, such as heat, drought, exposure to herbicides, attacks by pests or heavy rain.

Monsanto is facing an increasing number of lawsuits as its genetically engineered plants are not behaving as intended or promised. Many of the farmers who grew Monsanto's herbicide-tolerant cotton in 1997 were horrified as the cotton balls fell off their crops, which could be a sign of high stress or gene instability. In 1996, Monsanto's pest-resistant cotton (Nucotn) couldn't take the heat wave of the Southern US and found itself eaten alive by bollworms and their friends. About 50% of the fields needed emergency spraying with insecticides to salvage the crop.

When Plants Produce Pesticides

Getting plants to produce new pesticides causes other problems. Over 30 American groups, including farmers, environmentalists, scientists and consumer groups, are conducting a legal challenge against the Environmental Protection Agency in the US. The challenge is over the licensing of transgenic plants, which produce a toxin from the bacterium Bacillus thuringiensis (Bt).

Bt is a naturally occurring bacterium, which can be used as a biological pest-control product. The bacteria produce a chemical, which will turn into an active toxin when eaten by larvae of specific insects. Organic farmers have used these bacteria for over 50 years when pests threaten to devour their crops. Yet Bt cannot be sprayed on a proactive and regular basis as this will lead to resistance in many insects, rendering the bio-toxin useless to organic farmers. The use of Bt has already led to regional cases of resistance and such developments have been watched closely.

But now the usefulness of Bt is at stake. Modified toxin genes of different strains have been isolated and spliced into corn, potato, cotton, tomato, rape-seed, apple, tobacco, walnut and aubergine plants. As more and more crops are engineered to be pest-resistant, insects feeding on those plants cannot find a refuge. The constant exposure to Bt toxin either kills all the insects off or leads irreversibly to resistance. Both scenarios are highly undesirable. Insects are critical to the entire food chain. Many animals including birds, frogs and hedgehogs live on them.

Many scientists already acknowledge that Bt will become useless within 10 years, but biotech companies seem to care little—by then most of the patents on Bt-technology will have expired and they will have lost their lucrative monopoly. They'll simply seek to engineer and monopolize other defense systems.

This kind of behavior seams to imply that plant life and all other life on our planet is merely there to be experimented with. There seems to be an underlying belief that nature can be controlled. But what if it can't? What if the experiments go wrong? The attempt to create superraces of plants at the cost of biodiversity and locally adapted crop varieties puts the globe's food supply at severe risk. Genetic engineering is designed for intensive farming, and means big business. At a time when our environment is already suffering extreme stress we should avoid risking fragile balance or compounding our problems with genetic engineering.

Traditionally, the role of the genetic scientist is analogous to that of the naturalist who studies individual plant and animal species. The science of ecology takes a broader view and studies the relationship between different plants and animals, recognizing the complex inter-relationships that link everything on Earth to everything else. Perhaps now there is a need for a new science—gene-ecology. Such a science would study the complex relationships between genes in the body as well as their interaction with the inner and outer environment.

"Biotech foods [are] crucial to overcoming hunger for 800 million food-short residents of poor countries and preventing the deaths of six million children."

Genetically Engineered Crops Can Help People in Developing Nations

Dennis T. Avery

In the following viewpoint Dennis T. Avery argues that genetically engineered crops have increased yields and improved the lives of farmers in developed nations and will do so for farmers in developing nations as well. According to Avery, many of the world's scientists agree that these higher-yield genetically engineered crops are necessary to feed the world's hungry. Despite evidence of their safety, some continue to oppose genetically engineered crops, claims Avery, but the success of these crops will ultimately overcome unproven fears. Avery is director of the Hudson Institute's Center for Global Food Issues.

As you read, consider the following questions:

1. In Avery's view, what are some of the breakthroughs emerging from biotech labs?
2. According to Avery, what happened when small-scale Chinese farmers planted acreage with pest-resistant biotech cotton?
3. What is surprising about the activists opposed to bio-foods, in the author's opinion?

Whatever their antics, . . . scaremongers [activists who oppose the use of biotechnology] are fighting a futile, rearguard action in much of the world. Would that the same could be said for Europe, however.

Outside the Continent, transgenic crops have swept across the world more rapidly than any previous farming technology, mainly because they protect crops more effectively and use less pesticide. The world's farmers are likely to plant biotech crops in record number of acres [in 2000].

Most of the biotech plantings will be in the United States, where nearly 75 million acres will be devoted to corn, soybeans, canola and other crops. Argentina will plant 17 million acres, mostly corn and soybeans, and Canada 10 million acres, mostly canola. China, Australia, South Africa, Mexico, Romania and Ukraine also are planting transgenic crops.

Biotech Breakthroughs

The reason that the biotech acreage will increase is that new breakthroughs continue to emerge from the lab. Among the recent ones:

A new "super-rice" that incorporates a corn gene for a higher rate of photosynthesis. It yields 35% more grain per acre.

Frost-tolerant crops that will survive lower temperatures than traditional crops, meaning higher yields for Canada and Russia, and more twice-yearly harvests in the United States and China.

A natural substance (avidin, from egg whites), that when bred into crops will protect them from storage insects—thus eliminating the need for pesticides during crop storage.

One of the key biotech triumphs to date has been "golden rice" that should prevent the Vitamin A deficiency that blinds or kills millions of children each year in poor rice-eating countries. The new rice contains beta-carotene, as carrots do; the body converts the beta-carotene into Vitamin A. (Many of these afflicted areas are too poor to make carrots a regular part of their diet.)

Amidst all these discoveries, the European Union [EU] has embarked on a quixotic quest to explain why it should be allowed to block imports of transgenic foods under the "precautionary principle." This holds that authorities should bar a technology until there's proof that its not harmful.

To see how this would work in practice, look at the humble tomato, that American import that is now at the base of so many great European dishes. In early 1800s, both Europeans and Americans thought the tomato was poisonous because it was a relative of the deadly nightshade plant. The precautionary principle would have done away with the tomato, and along with it that tasty pasta dish you ate last night.

The Perspective of People in Developing Countries

Per Pinstrup-Andersen of the International Food Policy Research Institute asked participants in the Congressional Hunger Center seminar to think about biotechnology from the perspective of people in developing countries: "We need to talk about the low-income farmer in West Africa who, on half an acre, maybe an acre of land, is trying to feed her five children in the face of recurrent droughts, recurrent insect attacks, recurrent plant diseases. For her, losing a crop may mean losing a child. Now, how can we sit here debating whether she should have access to a drought-tolerant crop variety? None of us at this table or in this room [has] the ethical right to force a particular technology upon anybody, but neither do we have the ethical right to block access to it. The poor farmer in West Africa doesn't have any time for philosophical arguments as to whether it should be organic farming or fertilizers or GM [genetically modified] food. She is trying to feed her children. Let's help her by giving her access to all of the options. Let's make the choices available to the people who have to take the consequences."

Ronald Bailey, *Reason*, January 2001.

The EU says it is taking action because European consumers are frightened of the new technology—even though there is no proof that any of the foods are dangerous. This behavior runs afoul of the World Trade Organization Treaty, which demands scientific proof of danger to bar imports. But to this WTO objection, some French scientists have a ready response—they claim that some biotech foods have the potential for new allergies. But no approved biotech food has been found to cause allergies. One product that did was caught and stopped in the research process. If any allergen did get approved, of course, it would be quickly withdrawn.

In fact biotech researchers are working to take natural allergens out of wheat, milk and peanuts, which would free millions of people from the torment of these allergies. Biotechnology will reduce food allergies, not exacerbate them.

If EU officials really think that European consumers do not like these products, then there's no problem. Who would buy them? If Europe on the other hand is allowed to block imports for reasons of public fear, then fear campaigns could become trade barriers against virtually all imported products. Hong Kong could say that its consumers think French wines cause cancer and must therefore be banned. France might retaliate by saying Hong Kong textiles are made with "Frankenstein cotton" and must be banned in turn. Before we knew it, the much-discussed trend toward globalization could be pitched back into the high-tariff days of the 1930s. Perhaps another Great Depression would follow.

Saving Jobs and Feeding the Hungry

That would be tragic. Small-scale Chinese farmers are planting more than 700,000 acres with pest-resistant biotech cotton [in 2000], half of it from China's own labs. The biotech cotton needs no more than one pesticide spray per year, instead of the current 15. This new cotton is putting an extra $150 in profits per hectare into the pockets of one million Chinese farmers who now earn $500 to $1,000 per year. China says biotech cotton has single-handedly saved its biggest source of jobs. The cotton bollworm was developing resistance to pyrethroid insecticides and would have driven cotton production out of the country. China's cotton industry employs many millions of textile workers as wall as farmers—whose jobs were saved by biotech.

The Chinese also have genetically improved tomatoes, tobacco and cucumbers, and are actively researching biotech varieties of corn, wheat, and canola, along with many fruits and vegetables. Based on the Chinese experience, an Indian government committee has recommended that India plant its own biotech cotton varieties.

Norman Borlaug, who won the Nobel Peace Prize in 1970

for breeding the "miracle wheat" of the Green Revolution, is enthusiastic about biotech crops. He warns that organic farming could not feed more than four billion people—the world already has more than six billion—even if we plowed down all the forests on earth to create more farmland.

The world's most distinguished scientists agree with Mr. Borlaug in a new report issued by the academies of science of Brazil, China, India, Mexico, and the United States along with the Third World Academy of Sciences in Trieste, Italy and the British Royal Society. The report, released earlier this summer, calls biotech foods crucial to overcoming hunger for 800 million food-short residents of poor countries and preventing the deaths of six million children under five who currently die each year from malnutrition.

Surprisingly, the activists opposed to bio-foods are not protesting use of biotechnology in medicine, where new developments hold the promise of saving millions of people from AIDS, colon and breast cancer.

Ethically, of course, there's no justification for using biotechnology to help the sick, but not the hungry. Fortunately, the activists won't have to wrestle with that dilemma much longer. The march of progress already is leaving them behind in much of the world, and will soon in Europe as well.

"Unless the control of [genetically modified (GM) food] passes to the developing countries and their farmers, they may find themselves worse off if they use GM crops."

Genetically Engineered Crops Will Not Help Developing Nations

GeneWatch

In the following viewpoint GeneWatch, an organization whose goal is to ensure that genetic technologies are used in an ethical and safe manner, argues that unless people living in developing nations escape the poverty that keeps them from buying or producing the food they need, genetically modified (GM) crops will not help them. In fact, GeneWatch claims, GM crops may hurt poor farmers, who will go into debt trying to pay royalties to the corporations who own the patents on herbicide-resistant GM crops. Moreover, herbicide-resistant GM crops grown next to natural fields could contaminate the organic crops of poor farmers, leaving the crops even more vulnerable to crop-destroying weeds, GeneWatch maintains.

As you read, consider the following questions:

1. According to GeneWatch, in addition to poverty, what factors contribute to world hunger?
2. In the authors' opinion, what solutions will alleviate poverty and hunger?
3. To whom are the four multinational corporations who dominate GM research accountable, in the authors' view?

GeneWatch, "GM Crops: Bringing Hope to the Starving?" *GeneWatch UK*, December 2002. Copyright © 2002 by *GeneWatch UK*, www.genewatch.org. Reproduced by permission.

One good reason to promote genetically modifed (GM) foods would be if they could provide for the millions of people—mostly in developing countries—who suffer from starvation and malnutrition. The world's population is expected to increase from 6 billion today to 8 billion in 2020 so we will soon have increasingly larger numbers of people to feed. Some supporters of GM foods have claimed that by questioning GM foods, the science of GM will suffer, new GM crops will be delayed, and hunger prolonged. As we make our decision about GM crops, it is important to consider how our actions may affect others.

To decide whether GM food will be able to feed the hungry, we need to ask:

- Why are people going hungry in a world where there is more than enough food to feed everyone?
- What is needed to provide people with enough food?
- Are developments in GM crops likely to help?
- Could GM crops make things worse?

Why Are People Hungry?

The most important reason some people (even in developed countries) do not have enough to eat is poverty—they do not have the money to buy the food they need or the means to produce it themselves. Wars or environmental catastrophes—such as drought or flood—can cause serious crop failures, but although these are very visible, they do not cause as much hunger as poverty overall.

What Are the Solutions?

There is no single solution for every country and different things need to be done at all levels. Internationally, trade rules have to be changed so that developing countries can compete and not be swamped by produce from subsidised farmers in the developed world. Debt relief must be given so that countries can concentrate on growing food and not on exporting crops to pay interest on debts. Nationally, there has to be research into sustainable, affordable and appropriate farming. This should be publicly funded as it has to be about providing food, not profit. On a local level, farmers need to be able to sell their produce at a fair price. Systems that are adapted to local environmental conditions and ways of working are important for long-term food security.

Can GM Help?

It is clear that technological fixes are not the answer. In many cases, there are solutions that are available now. In poor countries, lack of vitamin A and other nutrients such as iron can cause illness and even death. Many thousands of children go blind and others die each year in developing countries because of a lack of vitamin A. The World Health Organisation's plan to eradicate vitamin A deficiency by 2000 failed because the political will to supply the supplements or a proper mixed diet did not exist. The biotechnology industry has produced GM rice with extra pro-vitamin A which is converted into vitamin A in the body. They argue that this 'golden rice' will help prevent deaths due to lack of vitamin A. The GM rice has not yet been proven to work and some people feel it is being used to blackmail people to accept GM foods when it should be quite easy to solve the problem in other ways.

Other developments, such as GM crops which are toler-

Addressing the Real Problems

The problem of hunger in developing countries is not caused by lack of genetic engineering to produce more food. In most countries where hunger is prevalent, there is an excess of staples—"the world already produces sufficient food, [writes N. Alexandratos]." Today, there is enough grain produced to provide every human being on the planet with thirty-five hundred calories a day. This estimate does not even count many other commonly eaten foods such as vegetables, beans, nuts, root crops, fruits, meat from grass-fed animals, and fish.

"The undernourished and the food-insecure persons are in these conditions because they are poor in terms of income to purchase food, or in terms of access to agricultural resources, education, technology, infrastructure, and credit to produce their own food, [says Alexandratos]." Even in rich countries there are urban and rural ghettos where poverty, not lack of food, is the problem.

Carl F. Jordan, *BioScience*, June 2002.

---

ant to herbicides, are not very relevant to poor farmers who cannot afford chemicals. Overall, it is the needs of the developed world which are driving research into GM foods. 80% of GM crop research and development is undertaken by four multi-national corporations—Syngenta, Monsanto, Bayer CropScience and Aventis—who are accountable to their shareholders and for whom poor people are not a very attractive market.

Will GM Make Things Worse?

If GM foods increased the gap between rich and poor, it would be one reason to reject them. To invest in GM, companies have insisted that they are given patents on the genes they use and the crops and seeds they develop. Patents give a monopoly to the inventor and they can charge royalties for use of their invention. Companies and governments of the developed world are now pushing developing countries to accept patents on genes and seeds. This will benefit the companies producing GM crops, but small farmers cannot pay the royalties involved. Patents also obstruct public institutes from developing GM crops that are relevant to developing countries because they have to obtain permission and make payments to the companies who own the patents. Monsanto controls almost 90% of GM cotton through the patents and companies they have acquired. Unless the control of GM passes to the developing countries and their farmers, they may find themselves worse off if they use GM crops.

Genetic contamination may be more of a problem for developing countries than for the developed world. Many crops have wild relatives growing close by and can cross-pollinate with them. In Britain, it is sugar beet and oilseed rape—two of the GM crops that may be grown here first—that have wild relatives which could be contaminated. In tropical countries, where many staple food crops evolved (such as rice, maize and potatoes), there is a greater potential for genetic contamination. Already, imported GM maize has contaminated native varieties in Mexico.

Periodical Bibliography

The following articles have been selected to supplement the diverse views presented in this chapter.

Dennis T. Avery	"Biotech Can Feed the World," *American Outlook Today*, August 7, 2000.
Ronald Bailey	"Dr. Strangelunch Or: Why We Should Learn to Stop Worrying and Love Genetically Modified Food," *Reason*, January 2001.
Ronald Bailey	"If It Ain't Broke, Don't Fix It," *Reason*, January 17, 2001.
John Beringer	"Keeping Watch over Genetically Modified Crops and Foods," *Lancet*, February 20, 1999.
Economist	"Genetically Modified Food: Far Less Scary Than It Used to Be," July 26, 2003.
Kevin Finneran	"What's Food Got to Do with It?" *Issues in Science and Technology*, Summer 2001.
Nancy Fitzgerald and Nicole Dyer	"Superfood or Double Trouble? Genetically Modified Foods Cook up a Sizzling Debate," *Scholastic Choices*, February 2002.
Carl F. Jordan	"Genetic Engineering, the Farm Crisis, and Hunger," *BioScience*, June 2002.
Danny Kohl	"GM Food—Another View," *Nation*, April 16, 2001.
Mark Lynas	"Don't Count Your GM Chickenfeed," *Ecologist*, July 2000.
Charles C. Mann	"Biotech Goes Wild," *Technology Review*, July/August 1999.
Iain Murray	"Environmental Scientists Must Stop Crying Wolf," *Financial Times*, September 17, 2003.
Robert Paarlberg	"The Global Food Fight," *Foreign Affairs*, May/June 2000.
Andrew Peters	"Attack of the Weird Plants!" *Science World*, January 11, 1999.
Bob Phelps	"Say 'No!' to Gene Tech's Bitter Harvest," *Habitat Australia*, June 1999.
Adam Piore et al.	"What Green Revolution?" *Newsweek*, September 15, 2003.
Robert B. Shapiro	"How Genetic Engineering Will Save Our Planet," *Futurist*, April 1999.

Devinder Sharma   "GM Foods: Toward an Apocalypse," July 20,
                         2003. www.countercurrents.org.

David Tribe   "GM Food: Secret Scientists or Obfuscatory
                         Opponents?" *Quadrant*, July 2000.

Lisa Turner   "Playing with Our Food," *Better Nutrition*, June
                         2000.

Paul D. Winston   "Gene Modification: Food for Thought,"
                         Business Insurance, June 26, 2000.

CHAPTER 4

How Should Genetic Engineering Be Regulated?

Chapter Preface

Most scientists concede that biomedical research using genetic engineering should proceed cautiously, but many fear that laws criminalizing these experiments are dangerous and represent a step backward for science. According to Paul Berg, who won the Nobel Prize in Chemistry for his work on recombinant DNA, "Criminalizing pure science is an absurd throwback to prohibitions on speaking out on scientific issues or new truths."

Throughout history, people have frequently reacted to advances in technology with fear, which in turn has often been followed by attempts to ban and sometimes make it a crime to use the new technology. In 1734 French philosopher Voltaire argued for experimental inoculation against smallpox. According to historian Alan Charles Kors, Voltaire asked French leaders to consider "the benefits to be gained by applying our knowledge of nature to the knowable and remediable causes of human suffering." In response, the French government consulted two well-respected authorities at the University of Paris: the Faculty of Medicine and the Faculty of Theology. According to Kors, the Faculty of Medicine believed that "[inoculation] would take us into uncharted and dangerous seas of innovation beyond the control of rightful authority. It would vitiate the sorts of traditions that had kept us decent and humane." The Faculty of Theology argued that inoculation was an attempt to play God. For them, Kors explains, "Inoculation was an act of hubris, a wanton and insolent human intrusion on God's domain, and if we crossed that line, how would we ever find our way back to our rightful place in the natural order?" As a result of these views, inoculating people against smallpox remained a crime in France until King Louis XV died of the disease on May 10, 1774, after which inoculations were allowed.

Arguments similar to those advocated by the Faculties of Medicine and Theology in eighteenth-century France have been made concerning genetic engineering, particularly biomedical research that utilizes cloning. In fact, laws have been proposed that make it a crime to use any form of human cloning, including therapeutic cloning. This biomedical technique involves the transplantation of the nucleus of a patient's cells into embryonic cells, which are then stimulated to reproduce, creating an oocyte. This embryo might then be used to create healthy cells to replace the patient's unhealthy ones. Genetic researchers hope to use this technique to cure debilitating diseases such as Parkinson's, Alzheimer's, and diabetes. Despite its potential to, using Voltaire's words, "relieve human suffering," therapeutic cloning would become a crime if Congress eventually passes the Human Cloning Prohibition Act of 2001, which, as of November 2003, had yet to be approved by the Senate. Under the act, anyone who performed or participated in human cloning could be imprisoned for up to ten years. Moreover, if cloning was conducted for "pecuniary gain," participants could pay a fine of not less than $1 million.

Kors and others who oppose such laws fear that the government will make the same mistake as that made by the French Crown. According to Kors, if the government criminalizes biomedical research such as therapeutic cloning, "We have criminalized the effort both to understand nature and to make that knowledge available to those who choose to use it voluntarily and peacefully. We have criminalized the pursuit of knowledge that could alleviate human agony."

Other commentators claim that the American people will not make such a mistake. Noretta Koertge, professor of the history and philosophy of science at Indiana University, is more optimistic. She contends, "Any attempt to undermine science will, in the long run, be unsuccessful in this country. Americans place too high a value on medical advances to stifle research in that area—or so I hope."

Whether or not laws criminalizing therapeutic cloning will unnecessarily impede scientific progress is subject to debate. The authors in the following chapter debate the appropriateness of cloning bans as well as other controversies surrounding the regulation of genetic engineering.

"Labelling of [genetically modified] food is necessary."

The Labeling of Genetically Engineered Food Should Be Mandatory

Y.G. Muralidharan

Genetically modified (GM) foods should be labeled because consumers have the right to be informed about products that may threaten their health, argues Y.G. Muralidharan in the following viewpoint. Moreover, Muralidharan claims, labeling gives consumers the choice to abstain from using products that threaten the environment, as GM foods are believed to do. Labeling requirements further protect consumers, Muralidharan maintains, because the companies that market the products will be accountable for the label's accuracy. Muralidharan is a writer and consumer advocate from India.

As you read, consider the following questions:

1. According to Muralidharan, what have surveys and studies in Australia and the United Kingdom revealed about consumers' views of food labeling?
2. In the author's opinion, what are the differences between positve and negative labeling?
3. What determines how a label should look, in the author's view?

Y.G. Muralidharan, "GM Foods: Consumers' Right to Know," *The Hindu Business Line*, www.thehindubusinessline.com, November 25, 2002. Copyright © 2002 by The Hindu Business Line. Reproduced by permission.

W ithin years of their introduction in the market, genet- ically modified organisms (GMO) have generated, of- ten acrimonious, debate among the industry, consumers, government, regulators and the civil society. Apart from is- sues relating to safety, need, and environmental impact of GMO, the question of providing information to the con- sumers has attracted much attention. No discussion on GMO can be complete without addressing the question of genetically engineering foods.

A Need for Mandatory Labels

Labelling food products is nothing new. Plenty of foodstuff is being labelled either voluntarily or due to some sort of regulation. A packet of chocolates, biscuits, ice-cream or a bottle of soft drink contains enough information. But when it comes to the question of GM [genetically modified] foods, the industry backtracks. Various surveys have shown that consumers do not want to buy a food without knowing how it is made or produced or what it contains.

For instance, a national government survey of consumers in Australia found that 89 per cent wanted labelling of ge- netically engineer[ed] tomato[s]. In the UK [United King- dom], a study for the Food and Drink Federation by a mar- ket research company found an almost unanimous (93 per cent) demand for clear labelling of products, which are the result of biotechnology.

To be protected against products, production processes and services that are hazardous to health or life, is the right given to consumers. Given the nature of GM food and the non- availability of sufficient data about its safety, consumers need to know what they are buying and eating. Consumers may not be willing to jeopardise long-term health and safety merely to allow corporations to rush new foods to the market.

The Rights of the Consumer

A framework of eight basic rights has been developed over the years to protect consumer welfare. These form the basis of legislation and advocacy worldwide. Every year, on March 15, groups use World Consumer Rights Day to advance these principles:

- The right to the satisfaction of basic needs;
- The right to safety;
- The right to be informed;
- The right to choose;
- The right to be heard;
- The right to redress;
- The right to consumer education;
- The right to health and sustainable environment;

—Consumers International, UK

Given the experience in developed countries in implementing various regulations about food safety, it appears that labelling of GM food is necessary. For example, in developed countries, the slaughter houses are monitored daily by inspectors, the fast-food chains that sell the hamburgers are licensed and inspected by local health departments. Yet, in the face of all these rules and regulations, children still get sick eating tainted hamburgers.

Making Choices

Probably, the most important justification for labelling GM foods is the consumers right to be informed. It also involves the right to choose and to make informed choices. It is true that information alone cannot guarantee safety. Yet, it facilitates understanding and the choice to buy or not to buy. Product labels perform an important social function—the communication between a seller and the consumer.

It is widely believed that GM crops can damage the environment, which threatens the consumers' right to health and sustainable environment. The demand for GM foodstuffs will ultimately determine what GM plants are planted. The mounting evidence about GM crops-related health and environmental risks provides a strong justification for mandatory labelling of GM foods. In such a situation, consumers may want to use their purchasing power to exercise a precautionary approach. This needs proper information about GM foods.

There is a growing concern among consumers about the religious and ethical principles being threatened by foods available in the market. Many consumers prefer not to use products created by transferring genetic material across species boundaries. Vegetarians voice concern about products containing animal material. Recently, the [Indian] Government amended the Prevention of Food Adulteration Act and made it compulsory for ice-creams to carry a label that it is vegetarian or non-vegetarian. There is a move to extend this rule to cover cosmetics and drugs.

The Opposition to Labels

However, the industry engaged in producing GM food is hesitant to fix labels on its products. Their argument is that GM foodstuffs are substantially equivalent. The theory of substantial equivalence allows corporations to produce novel food products and have them treated the same way as traditional pure foods. Some years back, when food irradiation technology was introduced, the industry came out with a similar argument.

It is argued that GM foodstuff do not differ significantly from other conventional food products. Therefore, they do not require labelling. In Europe, Australia and New Zealand, GM food producers have said that they will support labelling only when the GM food is different. More particularly, they say that the GM protein or DNA should be present in the final product.

Units producing GM foods argue that they are substantially equivalent when asked to label. Yet, they themselves say that their biologically-engineered products are different and unique when seeking to patent them. Labelling would lead to escalation in the cost of GM food. The costs of testing, segregating, certifying and labelling would be imposed on all the foods in the supply chain, from producers to food retailers. It would indirectly make a consumer pay more, including those indifferent to labels. Also, the industry feels that labelling of GM food would be a barrier to trade under the World Trade Organisation (WTO) agreement.

The Contents of the Label

In the background of the technology and risks involved in GM food, it is essential that the label contains more information in a consumer-friendly language. Despite efforts made at the highest fora such as Codex Alimentarious Commission (Codex), there is no consensus as to how or what should be the contents of a label for GM food.

GM product labels may be positive or negative. Positive labels are those which inform consumers that a product is genetically modified or contains GM stuff. These are compulsory labelling schemes, mostly framed by the governments. The European Union's compulsory labelling scheme falls into this category.

"No need to worry, trust us, you said. Unlabeled genetically engineered food is perfectly safe."

Bulbul. © 1999 by Bulbul. Reproduced by permission.

Negative labelling consists of 'GMO-free' labels. These labels inform consumers that a foodstuff is not genetically modified. Producers resort to negative labelling because they believe that it will boost up their sales. GM food labels may also be either process or product labels. Some experts felt that labels should contain information only about the food product itself, and not the process by which it is manufactured. A consumer has a right to information both about the process and product. The myth of "substantially equivalent" can be broken if the process labelling is adopted.

Laws Governing Labels

The European Commission enacted the EU [European Union] Novel Foods and Novel Food Ingredients Regulation which requires food to be labelled if:

- It differs from the equivalent familiar food due to a change in composition or nutritional value;
- Its consumption has health implications caused by allergens or other factors not present in the existing equivalent food;
- It creates ethical considerations (plant containing animal DNA);
- It consists of, or contains, a GMO.

Food must be approved and labelled before it is released into the market, and all food that consists of, or contains, GMOs must satisfy a detailed environmental risk and food safety assessment as a precondition to commercial release. The EU law applies equally to all GMO food, and does not discriminate on the basis of origin.

The Style of Disclosure

Assuming that labelling of GM food would be agreed upon by the industry, government and regulators, the question arises as to how should the label look . . . ? This depends on the purpose of labelling and [for] whom it is intended. . . . Naturally it is the consumers who need labelling. The difficulty arises in a country such as India where language, culture, rate of literacy, and so on, are to be considered.

Giving poor and illiterate consumers the required information about GM food poses several difficulties. First, it is language. This may be true in other developing countries as well. Instead, the label should consist of pictures, symbols and distinct marks.

Sustained efforts have to be taken to educate consumers about the symbols used and what they mean. Even after four decades, the ISI mark of the Bureau of Indian Standards, signifying minimum required quality, has not made significant effect on the consumers.

Who Is Accountable?

Selling or even storing a product without sufficient information or labels is not only unethical but also illegal. Throughout the world, there exists some rule or law which provides for disclosure of information about the foodstuff being sold to the consumers. A minimum set of information is to be provided.

For instance, in India, the Prevention of Food Adulteration Act, the Packaged Commodity Rules under the Weights and Measures Act and the Drugs and Cosmetics Act prescribe standards for disclosure of information.

If any product, particularly foodstuff and drugs are sold without the required information, it would be illegal and the manufacturer and seller are liable for fines. The object of these legislations is to protect consumers.

But the question is who would be liable in case a person suffers ill-effects after consuming GM foods? The answer depends on whether GM food itself is safe or not.

Studies have shown that GM foods may react on persons who are allergic. A person allergic to GM foods should necessarily avoid it. There are hundreds of cosmetics that are dangerous to consumers. Yet, they are sold in thousands. Knowing that smoking is injurious to health, lots of consumers smoke. So, who should be held responsible?

| *"Mandatory [genetically modified food] labelling is a bad idea."*

The Labeling of Genetically Engineered Food Should Not Be Mandatory

Gregory Conko

Mandatory labeling of genetically modified (GM) food would increase the cost of these products and generate unwarranted fear in consumers, claims Gregory Conko in the following viewpoint. Requiring that producers trace GM organisms at all stages of production would raise costs, which would be passed on to consumers. Moreover, Conko contends, labeling laws are inconsistent, making it impossible for consumers to know what products are truly free of genetic modification. Gregory Conko is director of food safety policy at the Competitive Enterprise Institute, a public policy organization dedicated to free enterprise and limited government.

As you read, consider the following questions:

1. Why are some products, such as oils from GM maize or soya, exempt from labeling requirements in Conko's view?
2. In the author's opinion, why is the cost of segregating GM from non-GM food not worth bearing?
3. According to Conko, what questionable distinction is made to exempt some foods from labeling?

Until mid-February 2003, the US government was readying a World Trade Organisation (WTO) challenge to the European Union (EU)'s moratorium on new GM [genetically modified] crop approvals. The EU hasn't approved any new GM varieties since 1998, and the two varieties that are approved have virtually disappeared from supermarket shelves due to consumer concerns.

European politicians have acknowledged that the moratorium may not withstand a WTO review. But they have suggested that the moratorium probably will be lifted in the next few months anyway—once new rules are in place for GM crops and foods.[1]

New Rules, Old Problems

Among the new rules—now being finalised by EU member states—is a requirement that GM foods be labelled and GM ingredients be 'traced' through the food chain, from plant-breeder and farmer, to shipper, processor and retailer. EU politicians boast that their health, environment and labelling rules comprise 'the toughest GM legislation in the world', and tout them as just the trick to restore public confidence in food biotechnology.

Although GM food labelling is already mandatory, advocates claim that the stronger new labelling and traceability rules will ensure that consumers have more complete information, enabling them to make informed choices. In truth, the measures will do no such thing.

Both the existing and the proposed labelling regulations only require certain categories of GM foods to be labelled, and provide no context for why some are to be labelled and others exempt. So to make truly informed choices, shoppers must rely upon other sources of information. It is more likely that mandatory labelling will merely raise the cost of GM products, and add to many consumers' groundless fears about GM foods.

Consider the existing European Commission 'novel foods' regulation and the Council of the European Commu-

---

1. Laws were passed in July 2003 that should allow EU member nations to end the moratorium.

nities GM labelling regulation, which came into effect in 1997 and 1998 respectively. These require any food or animal feed to be labelled if DNA or proteins from a GM organism can be detected in the final product.

In practice, products like oils from GM maize or soya usually do not have to be labelled, because heat from the crushing process breaks apart DNA chains and breaks down proteins, making it impossible to tell the difference between GM and non-GM oils. Consequently, some GM-derived products—including cooking oils, maize sweetener, and the soy lecithin in chocolate—still appear unlabelled on supermarket shelves.

Misleading, Not Informing Consumers

In every country where mandatory GM food labelling has occurred or is in development, regulators have allowed for an extensive network of exemptions and loopholes in order to make such labelling practical and comparatively inexpensive. As a result, many food ingredients that are obtained from GM crops are exempted, and foods that are classified as 'non-GM' may actually contain a significant percentage of ingredients that come from GM sources. Consumers who buy such foods on the basis of their 'non-GM' classification are being seriously misled.

Ontario Corn Producers Association, *OCP Magazine*, November 2001.

Some see this as a flaw in the current laws, which will be remedied by new rules expanding the labelling requirement. Under these regulations, foods and animal feed will have to be labelled if they are produced from a GM organism, regardless of whether or not the end product can be distinguished from conventionally produced items. To facilitate this change in policy, seed breeders, farmers, shippers, processors and retailers will be required to keep detailed records of GM products so they can be traced all the way through the food chain.

The Cost of Labelling

Nearly two billion metric tons of cereal grains are grown in the world every year. And the food supply's continued affordability depends upon the commoditisation process, in which shippers treat all maize, soya and wheat alike. To shippers, food processors and, more importantly, the human body itself, maize is maize whether it is harvested in Britain, France or the USA, and whether it is grown from GM or conventional plants.

Segregating genetically modified organisms (GMOs) out of the commodity stream to comply with the traceability requirement would disrupt this efficient process, at immense cost. Moreover, perfect compliance would be impossible. The traceability provision could raise the bar for GM products so high that the market would abandon them—a point that may have motivated GM opponents to support labelling.

Of course, if the strict segregation of GM from non-GM were necessary to protect consumer health, such a cost might be worth bearing. But these measures are not necessary, because there isn't a single identifiable risk of genetic modification that doesn't also exist with one or another form of conventional breeding. And the fact that GM foods are now commercially available in EU member states—and will be available even after implementation of the new GM rules— shows that the driving force for labelling is not concern for consumer health.

Making Questionable Distinctions

Labelling supporters counter that there may be unidentifiable risks, and that their goal is simply to provide consumer choice. How, then, do supporters explain provisions in both the current and proposed labelling schemes that exempt entire classes of GM foods from the labelling mandate?

The distinction revolves around the seemingly innocuous phrase 'produced from GM'. That is, if oil is produced from GM maize, or if tofu is produced from GM soya, then the final product is also considered to be genetically modified and must be labelled. However, foods that are 'produced with' a GMO—including cheeses produced with the aid of the GM clotting-agent chymosin, or wines and beers produced with GM yeasts—are not considered to be genetically modified and need not be labelled, even though residues of the GMOs often remain in the final products.

And animal feeds must be labelled if they are produced

'from' GM grains, providing a choice for farmers and their livestock. But meat from animals fed GM food is exempt—human consumers have less choice. If unanticipated or unidentifiable risks are the problem that makes labelling necessary, why exempt so many obviously 'GM foods'?

Perhaps it is because there is so much disagreement over what really is and is not genetically modified—some GM critics have opposed the labelling and traceability rules because they are too lax. Or perhaps it is because European politicians are trying to carve out an exemption for domestically produced wines, beers and cheeses, while erecting an almost insurmountable barrier against imported grains.

Whatever the motivation, mandatory GM labelling is a bad idea. And one of the most compelling arguments against it is that European consumers will not be able to rely upon information provided to them. This or any other political solution will necessarily be a compromise that takes too long to implement, too long to change, and leaves too many unsatisfied. There is, however, another option.

The Advantages of Negative Labelling

Already, thousands of negatively labelled non-GM foods appear on shop shelves throughout the EU. Why? Because information has value, and like other valuable items, consumer demand can drive producers to make it available to those who genuinely want it. As we see in the case of GM foods, that information doesn't necessarily come in the form of labelled GM products. But it can, and does often come in the form of labelling designed to attract consumers who want certain attributes.

Label information about GM status is primarily used by those trying to avoid GM foods. Consequently, a vibrant market has developed for foods negatively labelled as 'GMO-free' or 'organic'. No mandate was necessary. Because they must compete for the attention of shoppers, food packagers and supermarkets long ago responded to consumer demand for non-GM products—and they did so with labelling policies that are actually better at providing real consumer choice.

| *"There are many . . . reasons why all human cloning should be banned."*

All Forms of Human Cloning Should Be Banned

Robert A. Best

According to Robert A. Best in the following viewpoint, originally given as testimony to the U.S. House Subcommittee on Oversight and Investigations on March 28, 2001, all forms of human cloning, whether to reproduce a human being (reproductive) or to conduct medical research (therapeutic), should be banned. All embryos, at any stage of their development, are human beings, and to experiment on them is a violation of their rights, claims Best. Moreover, he maintains, human cloning perverts the nature of parent-child relationships, gives people God-like power over others, and deprives cloned individuals of human dignity. Best is president of the Culture of Life Foundation and Institute, whose goal is to protect all human life from conception until natural death.

As you read, consider the following questions:

1. In Best's opinion, what code, established after the trials of Nazi leaders at the close of World War II, does human cloning violate?
2. According to the author, what strategy do scientists who want to experiment on human embryos use to evade the question of whether cloning is ethical?
3. What trend does human cloning increase that the author believes needs to be reversed?

Robert A. Best, testimony before the U.S. House Subcommittee on Oversight and Investigations, Committee on Commerce and Energy, Washington, D.C., March 28, 2001.

There are many reasons why human cloning in all forms should be prohibited, but one that relates closely to your Constitutional role [as elected representatives] is that human cloning attacks the understanding of equality, which is the organizing principle of our Republic. The equality clause of the Declaration of Independence and the concept of "one person, one vote" lose their meaning when human persons become manufactured products. In other words, a democracy that permits human cloning will not remain one for very long.

I know the [House] Subcommittee [on Oversight and Investigations] will look carefully at the question of cloning for therapeutic purposes, in other words the creation by cloning of human embryos which are used for research in the embryonic stage (resulting in their destruction) or are developed into a fetal stage, used for research, and then killed prior to birth. Even if such a practice were not lethal to the embryo or fetus, it would still be objectionable in terms of the moral and ethical tradition of this country. Research on cloned embryos and fetuses, like research on any other human embryos and fetuses, would constitute medical experimentation on human persons without their individual voluntary consent, and would violate the Nuremberg Code. This Code, enunciated following the trials of Nazi leaders at the close of World War II, is not a law or a treaty obligation. But the Code is a fair summary of the civilized ethical standard of experimentation on living human beings.

The Embryo Is a Human Being

Mister Chairman, the embryo may not look it, but it is a human being. Whether by cloning or by the fertilization of an egg by sperm, the resulting embryo is a new and unique human being with its genetic identity in place and the capability, properly protected and nurtured, to become as apparently independent as you or I. Some say the need for protection and nurturing invalidates the embryo's claim to humanity, but which of us, at any stage of life, does not require protection and nurturing? The only difference is of degree, and if we accord human rights only to those who are substantially free of the need for protection and nurturing by others, then many people in hospitals and nursing homes and supersonic airliners and space stations and at this moment in the Metro tunnel under the Potomac between Foggy Bottom and Roslyn are not human beings, either.

Mr. Chairman, there is nothing "therapeutic" about killing a human being, even in the earliest stages of life. "Therapeutic," according to my Webster, means "to serve, take care of, treat medically, . . . of or pertaining to healing." The proponents of human cloning have masked their mission of killing one human being or group of human embryos to "create" another human being. Whatever their motives, there is no moral justification for killing an innocent human being. Once we go down that road, life becomes cheap, culture become coarse, killing becomes thrilling or "therapeutic."

Mr. Chairman, we as a nation dare not go down that road. The precedents for using human beings as fodder for creating the "perfect" human being resulted in disaster for more than one nation in the twentieth century. German scientists and the medical profession of that nation created a climate in which they determined which life was "worth living," the ultimate arrogance. By the time Hitler came to power, the medical profession in Germany had already engaged in massive killing of innocents for the sake of a "pure race." The culture of death started in Germany long before Hitler came to power; he turned a culture of death against the Jews and others whom he deemed unworthy of living.

At the dawn of a new millennium, we must see in every human being someone precious and worthy of our love. The Pope, who lived under both the Nazis and the Communists, has called out for a culture of life. To foster a culture that loves life is not a partisan or even a "religious" cause; it is a human cause that Democrats, Republicans, Independents and all people of good will should aspire to and champion.

The Justification for Experimentation

Those who want to conduct experiments that involve the killing of human embryos understand the issue, and therefore seek to call embryos by some other name, at least for the duration of the experiment. Thus some maintain that no human embryos should be termed as such during their first two weeks of existence. Terms like "totipotent cell," "clump of embryonic cells," and "unfertilised oocyte" are used to evade the issue. However, the scientific data are clear: a successful somatic cell nucleus transfer to a de-nucleated egg creates an embryo.

Experimentation on embryos and fetuses turns human beings into spare parts sources and test beds for other human beings. Such experimentation not only kills individuals, and is therefore cruel, but it also denigrates the dignity of being human by bringing a person into existence and then manipulating him or her for one's own purpose. The advocates of such use of human embryos and fetuses describe the suffering caused by defects and diseases which might be cured by their experiments, but adult stem cells, which are freely available without killing or manipulating anyone, have shown more promise thus far than have either embryonic stem cells or fetal tissue.

Let me be clear: good cannot come from a bad action. Even the most dire human suffering would not justify the involuntary death of another human being, embryonic, fetal, or ambulatory. But the promise of adult stem cells may obviate even this insufficient but emotionally strong argument for lethal experimentation on human embryos and fetuses.

Perverting Human Relationships

There are many other reasons why all human cloning should be banned, and I stress that these reasons are practical, not theoretical, and are based on universal truths. First, cloning changes the nature and meaning of human sexuality. If a new person can be produced by taking the nucleus of a somatic cell from a man and injecting it into the de-nucleated oocyte of a woman, then human sexuality becomes superfluous. From its age-old purpose of transforming human love into new life, sexuality in an age of cloning would become, even more than it has unfortunately already become, simply an itch to scratch. We have seen in the past half-century, as the connection between sexuality and reproduction has weakened in the "sexual revolution," a rise in negative social indicators such as divorces, abortions, an explosion of sexually transmitted diseases including one that is 100% fatal, and greatly increased exploitation of women in prostitution and pornography. By further weakening sexuality's reproductive purpose, cloning would therefore further weaken families and communities.

Second, human cloning would weaken or even pervert basic human relationships such as family, fatherhood and motherhood, consanguinity, and kinship. For example, if a clone resulted from the nucleus of a somatic cell taken from his "father", his biological tie to his "mother" would be vastly different than that of a natural child. Apart from mitochondria DNA, which is outside the nucleus and is always passed on the maternal side, the clone would inherit no characteristics, no other DNA, no genetic material, from his mother. This very different biological tie could contribute to a different emotional mother-son tie as well. Further, as the clone would likely be "the spitten image" of his father, the mother's already different relationship with her child would become truly bizarre. Human cloning therefore perverts the relationships that are fundamental to our mental health and to the health of society.

Sacrificing Human Freedoms

Third, human cloning would compromise the dignity of the cloned person because she would forever know she was biologically identical to another person. Richard Seed, a scientist who wants to set up a cloning clinic in the U.S., has reportedly said that he wished he could have obtained a blood sample from Mother Teresa from which to clone a saint. Of course, the resulting little girl would only be *biologically* identical to Mother Teresa. Her own environment and experiences would make her a unique person. But the expectations that others would put on that child, and the expectations she would place on herself, would make for a miserable life. She would have lost the essential human freedom to be oneself. The children of the famous and notorious sometimes carry a heavy burden, but at least they retain the freedom of their own individuality. The cloned person would have lost that basic freedom because of the decision of another person.

The threat of power over others is a fourth reason to oppose human cloning. Most parents consciously choose to have children, and some try to influence the development of their child *in utero*. All responsible parents exercise authority over their children after birth and use their authority to educate and develop their children. This use of parental authority is natural. But human cloning gives a person absolute dominion over the existence of another. Whether the person comes into existence at all, when the person comes into existence, what the person's genetic material will be, what the person's intelligence and appearance and special skills will be—all this would be determined by another person. As I noted earlier, if people can have this kind of power over others, than the equality clause is just empty words from a quaint past. Those who would clone people seek a dominion over others which can only be termed "Godlike." Like the bypassing of human sexuality to achieve reproduction, the calling into existence of a precisely specified new person is an exercise in apparent human omnipotence.

A Distinction Without a Difference

The question of cloning "whole human beings" in reproductive cloning, as distinct from therapeutic cloning [used in medical research and procedures], is a distinction without a difference from a moral point of view. The particular future of an embryo does not make a difference to its status as a human being. In both therapeutic and reproductive cloning a human being is engendered who is a legitimate bearer of human rights. The fact that in one case and not in the other the embryo is allowed to progress into later stages of development, or that an estimated 50–80% of embryos in natural gestation never implant and die, or that the embryo prevented from implanting is destined to die, do not make an essential difference to whether the embryo is, *per se*, a human being.

Peter J. Cataldo, testimony before the Senate Committee on Science and Technology, Commonwealth of Massachusetts, December 12, 2001.

A fifth reason to oppose human cloning is that it will increase a trend which we need to reverse, if we want to retain our freedom: the trend toward evaluating other people on the basis of their qualities instead of on their existence. Human cloning will always be the outcome of a choice about the specific traits and qualities of a child. As we have seen, cloning turns human reproduction into a manufacturing process. In time, given our national genius at capitalism, particular qualities and the raw material needed to obtain them will be available in exchange for money. Health insurers, for example, have a financial incentive to favor healthier children. Wealthy parents will use cloning to get ever-higher "quality" children ("quality" meaning whatever the fashion of the time dictates) while poor people, reproducing in the traditional way, would lag ever farther behind. Again, the strain imposed on our concept of equality will be too much, and self-government will end.

The Medical Risks of Cloning

I said earlier that human cloning would be an exercise in apparent human omnipotence. I say "apparent" because, unlike the natural reproductive system which has brought us to this point, cloning is fraught with physical risks. Many of those risks have already been displayed in the cloning of mammals. For example, Dolly the cloned sheep was the one live birth derived from 277 sheep embryos which were created in the experiment. Cloned embryos appear to develop into larger-than-normal fetuses, resulting in a high incidence of still-births and Caesarean section deliveries. Developmental problems associated with abnormal size of human clones would include a high incidence of death in the first few weeks from heart and circulatory problems, diabetes, under-developed lungs, or immune system problems. The January death from a common infection of a cloned wild gaur (an endangered South Asian species) at Trans-Ova Genetics in Sioux Center, Iowa, may indicate that cloned animals have a lower resistance to disease. Another problem is the potential for clones to have aging DNA and thus an accelerated aging process. Lord Robert Winston, one of the developers of in vitro fertilization, has stated that because of the faster aging process, he would not want a child of his to be cloned.

The current low rate of cloning success with mammals (two clones born per 100 implantations, according to one source, up to 17 per 100 according to another) suggests a similarly low success rate for human cloning. And even if a seemingly normal and healthy animal is born, a defect that was not apparent can suddenly cause death, as was the case with a cloned sheep born last December at the same center which produced Dolly. The March 25, 2001, *New York Times*, reporting on the cloning of animals, described a high rate of spontaneous abortion and post-natal developmental delays, heart defects, lung problems, and malfunctioning immune systems among cloned animals who had initially seemed normal. But let us stipulate that human ingenuity will gradually increase the success rate: who could live with having caused the pain of the many human clones who suffered and died along the way?

Mister Chairman, for these many reasons the Culture of Life Institute urges you to protect the lives of an untold number of individuals and to protect the principle of equality which is the basis of our legal and governmental system by drafting and passing a bill which would prohibit the cloning of human beings, at any stage of development, for any purpose.

"[The prohibition of human cloning] would tragically limit biomedical research."

Some Forms of Human Cloning Should Not Be Banned

Rudolf Jaenisch

Reproductive cloning is used to reproduce an entire organism whereas therapeutic cloning is used to create cells and tissues used in medical research. Therapeutic cloning, which could benefit patients with debilitating diseases, should not be banned, argues Rudolf Jaenisch in the following viewpoint, which was originally given as testimony to the Senate Subcommittee of Science, Technology and Space on May 2, 2001. Using therapeutic cloning techniques, claims Jaenisch, doctors will eventually be able to create healthy cells to replace defective cells in patients with diseases such as Parkinson's and Alzheimer's. The federal government should not ban an area of scientific exploration such as therapeutic cloning to assuage unknown fears when the potential benefits are so great, he contends. A professor of biology and a research scientist, Jaenisch is a member of the American Society for Cell Biology.

As you read, consider the following questions:

1. According to Jaenisch, what is the most likely cause of abnormal development in animal clones?
2. In the author's opinion, what has research using the embryonic stem cells of a mouse been able to demonstrate?
3. What did scientists do twenty-five years ago when they were at a crossroads with recombinant DNA technology, according to the author?

Rudolf Jaenisch, testimony before the U.S. Senate Subcommittee of Science, Technology and Space, Committee on Commerce, Science and Transportation, Washington, D.C., May 2, 2001.

I am Rudolf Jaenisch and I am here today [May 2, 2001] as a representative of the American Society For Cell Biology [ASCB]. The Society represents more than 10,000 basic biomedical researchers throughout the United States and the world, most of whom work in our Nation's leading research universities and institutes. It is my pleasure to appear before you today.

I am a founding Member of the Whitehead Institute and Professor of Biology at MIT. Before coming to the Whitehead Institute I was the head of the Department of Tumor Virology at the Heinrich Pette Institute of the University of Hamburg in Germany. I am privileged to have helped establish the field of transgenic science. Transgenic science deals with the transfer of genes to create mouse models of human disease.

A Critical Distinction

On March 28 [2001], I testified before the House Subcommittee on Oversight and Investigations at a hearing entitled "Issues Raised by Human Cloning Research." There I emphasized the scientific concerns of human cloning that have resulted from the problems encountered in animal cloning. Our experience with animal cloning allows us to predict with a high degree of confidence that few cloned humans will survive to birth and, of those, the majority will be abnormal. The most likely cause of abnormal clone development is faulty reprogramming of the genome. This may lead to abnormal gene expression of any of the 30,000 genes residing in the animal. Faulty reprogramming does not lead to chromosomal or genetic alterations of the genome, so methods that are used in routine prenatal screening to detect chromosomal or genetic abnormalities in a fetus cannot detect these reprogramming errors. There are no available methods now or in the foreseeable future to assess whether the genome of cloned embryo has been correctly reprogrammed. The ASCB stated in 1998 its clear opposition to the cloning of a human being and remains a steadfast opponent today.

There is, however, a critical distinction between the cloning of a human being—which is both morally questionable and scientifically dangerous—and the therapeutic cloning of cells for the purpose of developing tissue that may ultimately allow defective cells in people to be replaced by healthy cells. The Human Cloning Prohibition Act of 2001 prohibits the use of somatic cell nuclear transfer for the purposes of human cloning. This undoubtedly intended to prevent the cloning of a human being, but it also, perhaps inadvertently, would tragically limit biomedical research. Therapeutic cloning has the capability to turn human cells into specific tissue types, for example, to regenerate nerve cells and heart muscle cells, benefiting patients with Parkinson's, Alzheimer's and heart disease. The potential benefits of therapeutic cell cloning are indisputable—the only uncertainty is when they will be realized.

The Promise of Stem Cells

Public reaction to animal cloning and the disreputable threats of human cloning are in grave danger of hindering critical research in embryonic stem [ES] cells for the repair of organs and tissues. Just over a year ago, a milestone in biomedical research was achieved when human embryonic stem lines were obtained by growing cells from the inner cell mass of early stage human embryos. Research work over the past 20 years using mouse embryonic stem cells has demonstrated the promise of these cells for basic research and potential disease therapy. ES cells by themselves cannot form a mouse, but they can differentiate into any of the cell types that comprise a mouse. Mouse ES cells have been used to elucidate many important aspects of normal mouse embryology and development, but, most important, mouse ES cells are currently being used in a variety of "proof of therapeutic principle" experiments in several animal models of human disease. For example, these cells appear to be able to produce neural progenitors that can repair spinal cord damage and reconstitute brain cells that produce the chemicals that control cognition, motion and sensory perception. If reproducible with human ES cells, this could lead to effective treatment of Parkinson's disease and Alzheimer's disease. Similarly, the production of healthy bone marrow cells to treat cancer and other hematopoietic diseases, and pancreatic cells to alleviate diabetes are all within reach, so long as

well-intentioned efforts to prevent the cloning of human beings—living, talking, feeling, walking around human beings—do not unintentionally interfere.

Stem Cells' Unlimited Potential

Researchers believe that human embryonic stem cells can be
grown into a variety of body parts, enabling them to fight
many common afflictions.

Cells Derivable from Stem Cells	Target Diseases
Insulin-producing cells	Diabetes
Nerve cells	Stroke, Parkinson's disease, Alzheimer's disease, Spinal cord injury
Heart muscle cells	Heart attacks, Congestive heart failure
Liver cells	Hepatitis, Cirrhosis
Blood cells	Cancer, Immunodeficiencies
Bone cells	Osteoporosis
Cartilage cells	Osteoarthritis
Eye cells	Macular degeneration
Skin cells	Burns, Wound healing
Skeletal muscle cells	Muscular dystrophy

Geron Corp., 1999.

We may be on the cusp of a new era of medicine, one in
which cell therapy could restore normal function to a variety
of affected tissues using stem cells. To understand the need
for rapid research progress with human pluripotent stem
cells, one need look no further than many common, and often fatal, diseases such as cancer, heart disease and kidney disease. These diseases are treatable in whole or in part by tissue or organ transplants, but there are persistent and deadly
problems of rejection and a woefully inadequate supply of
suitable donor organs and tissues. In addition, the grim arith-

metic of most organ transplants requires those who are seriously ill to wait for the tragic accidental death of another person so that they may live. Worse, for juvenile diabetes and many other diseases, there is not even a suitable transplantation therapy or other cure. Unless we use federal funds for all aspects of human pluripotent stem cell research new treatments for these conditions may be delayed by years, and many who might otherwise have been saved will surely die or endure needless suffering.

The Risks of a Ban

Cloning is an extremely complex area of biology in which the process itself is only now beginning to be understood. It is premature to ban a technique that is still in the process of evolving. At no point in our nation's history has Congress banned an area of scientific exploration or technology by federal legislation. We were at a similar crossroads 25 years ago with recombinant DNA technology, which indeed, as predicted, revolutionized science by spawning biotechnology and all of its medical and economic returns to this country. There is widespread support of the National Bioethics Advisory Commission's call for a voluntary international moratorium on human nuclear transfer for the purpose of creating a new human being. In addition, the Food and Drug Administration has specifically claimed that clinical research using cloning technology to create a human being is subject to FDA regulation under the Public Health Service Act and the Federal Food, Drug and Cosmetic Act. The ASCB urges that if legislation is needed, it should specifically be concerned with the reproduction of a human being by nuclear transfer. At the same time, any legislation should not impede or interfere with existing and potential critical research fundamental to the prevention or cure of human disease. This research often includes the cloning of human and animal cell lines and DNA, but not whole human beings.

"It would indeed be utterly unjust not to grant a patent to a scientist for a gene he worked to discover, isolate, and find a use for."

Scientists Should Be Allowed to Patent Genes

David Holcberg

According to David Holcberg in the following viewpoint, scientists who discover and isolate genes should be able to obtain patents. A natural substance is patentable, he claims, when it is isolated, purified, and found to have utility; the very process many gene researchers are using. Patents reward the work it takes to isolate a gene, Holcberg claims, thus to deny them to scientists would be unfair and would discourage scientific research. Holcberg, a former civil engineer, is a senior writer for the Ayn Rand Institute, an organization whose philosophy is to champion individual rights and the power of reason.

As you read, consider the following questions:
1. What value does an isolated gene have that it did not have before it was isolated, in Holcberg's view?
2. According to Holcberg, why was Louis Pasteur able to patent his yeast?
3. In the author's opinion, how was the principle that patents are appropriate for isolated natural substances purified when adrenaline was isolated?

On October 2000, I argued in "Who Owns Your Genes?" that naturally occurring genes should not be patented because they are not inventions, but discoveries of what already exists in nature. On January 2001, the U.S. Patent and Trademark Office (PTO) issued its guidelines for patents on genes and proved me wrong.

The PTO argued that "an isolated and purified DNA molecule that has the same sequence as a naturally occurring gene is eligible for a patent because that DNA molecule does not occur in that isolated form in nature."

Discovering Isolated Genes

The PTO's argument is that in discovering and isolating a gene, a scientist creates something that has never existed before: the isolated gene. A patent is therefore given as recognition that a gene, once identified, isolated, and shown to have a specific utility, acquires commercial value, value that it did not have before. Only then can it be manipulated and used for commercial purposes. And the same line of reasoning goes for any other material or substance that is discovered in nature and isolated from its source. In fact, the PTO observes that "patenting compositions or compounds isolated from nature follows well-established principles, and is not a new practice."

Consider some historical precedents that support the PTO's argument.

In 1873, for example, Louis Pasteur received a patent for "yeast, free from organic germs of disease, as an article of manufacture." Yeast had existed for thousands, if not millions of years before Pasteur developed an interest in it. But before Pasteur's investigations, yeast had never been processed to be free of germs. Pasteur created disease-free yeast, and properly received a patent for it.

Another precedent is a patent given for adrenaline. The patent was challenged in court in 1911 on the grounds that adrenaline was not invented but discovered. The court's decision affirmed the patent's validity and explained why it did so: "[Jokichi] Takamine was the first to make [adrenaline] available for any use by removing it from the other gland-tissue in which it was found, and, while it is of course possible logically to call this a purification of the principle, it became for every practical purpose a new thing commercially and therapeutically. That was a good ground for a patent." The court's point was that adrenaline, as well as any other substance, should be patentable "even if it were merely an extracted product without change."

The PTO reiterates the court's point in defense of its own guidelines: "Like other chemical compounds, DNA molecules are eligible for patents when isolated from their natural state and purified or when synthesized in a laboratory from chemical starting materials."

Living Is Not Infringement

But if isolated genes identical to genes in our own bodies can be patented, wouldn't we be violating their patents just by being alive and making use of our genes in our metabolic processes?

No, argued the PTO. "A patent on a gene covers the isolated and purified gene but does not cover the gene as it occurs in nature. Thus, the concern that a person whose body includes a patented gene could infringe the patent is misfounded. The body does not contain the patented, isolated and purified gene because genes in the body are not in the patented, isolated and purified form. When the patent [was] issued for purified adrenaline about one hundred years ago, people did not infringe the patent merely because their bodies naturally included unpurified adrenaline."

In light of the PTO's clear case for the propriety of patenting genes, I am glad that my arguments did not prevail. It would indeed be utterly unjust not to grant a patent to a scientist for a gene he worked to discover, isolate, and find a use for.

Historically, patents have been a huge incentive to inventors, researchers, and businessmen who, in the absence of patents, would not have invested so much of their time, effort and capital in their endeavors. If we want progress in medical research and treatment to continue we must keep in mind that granting patents for genes is not only practical, but moral as well.

Periodical Bibliography

The following articles have been selected to supplement the diverse views presented in this chapter.

Mohamed Larbi Bougerra — "Genes of Inequality," *UNESCO Courier*, September 1999.

Karen Charman — "Spinning Science into Gold," *Sierra*, July 2001.

Marcy Darnovsky — "Embryo Cloning and Beyond," *Tikkun*, July/August 2002.

Kristin Dawkins — "Unsafe in Any Seed: U.S. Obstructionism Defeats Adoption of International Biotechnology Safety Agreement," *Multinational Monitor*, March 1999.

Steven M. Druker and L. Val Giddings — "At Issue: Should All Genetically Engineered Foods Be Labeled?" *CQ Researcher*, September 4, 1998.

Economist — "The Great Cloning Debate: Biology and Politics," May 11, 2002.

Francis Fukuyama — "In Defense of Nature, Human and Non-Human," *World Watch*, July/August 2002.

Dinyar Godrej — "Eight Things You Should Know About Patents on Life," *New Internationalist*, September 2002.

Richard Hayes — "The Science and Politics of Genetically Modified Humans," *World Watch*, July/August 2002.

Tony Juniper — "Consumers' Right to Choose GM-Free Food," *Spiked*, February 27, 2003.

Jonathan King and J. Craig Venter — "At Issue: Does Patenting Human Genes Impede Medical Research?" *CQ Researcher*, May 12, 2000.

Arlene Judith Klotzko — "A Cloning Emergency in Britain?" *Scientist*, January 7, 2002.

Jane Maienschein — "Who's in Charge of the Gene Genie?" *World & I*, January 2000.

Henry I. Miller — "EPA Disregards Science: New Biotech Rules Not Based on Risk," *Consumers' Research*, August 2001.

Henry I. Miller — "FDA Clones Misguided Regulatory Policy," *Scientist*, July 9, 2001.

Chris Mooney

"The Future Is Later: The Cloning Fight Comes Down to Abortion—and Down to Earth," *American Prospect*, July 15, 2002.

Virginia Postrel, ed.

"Criminalizing Science: Leading Thinkers and Commentators Respond to a Left-Right Alliance to Outlaw 'Therapeutic Cloning' and Stigmatize Genetic Research," *Reason*, November 2001.

Judy Rebick

"Attack of the Tomato People," *Herizons*, Fall 2001.

Seth Shulman

"Toward Sharing the Genome," *Technology Review*, September/October 2000.

Gregory Stock

"Go Ahead and Clone," *Reason*, March 18, 2002.

For Further Discussion

Chapter 1

1. Henry I. Miller and Gregory Conko argue that biotech companies use genetic engineering to help cure diseases and feed the hungry. Ronnie Cummins argues that biotech companies will use genetic engineering to dominate global markets without concern for public safety. These authors have distinctly different views about the motives of biotech companies. Which view, in your opinion, is supported by more convincing evidence? Explain.

2. Jeremy Rifkin opposes human cloning because it takes reproduction out of the hands of individuals and places it in the hands of the corporate elite. James A. Byrne and John B. Gurdon argue, however, that barring human cloning would result in a diminution of individuals' reproductive choices. Citing evidence from the viewpoints, explain whose position you find more persuasive.

3. Judith Levine distinguishes the choice to terminate a pregnancy from the choice to select a child's genetic traits. George Dvorsky disputes that distinction, arguing that genetic selection is no different from the choices women already make to optimize the health of their children, including the termination of a fetus shown during prenatal screening to have a genetic disease. Do you think there is a distinction between terminating a pregnancy and genetic selection? Explain, citing from the viewpoints.

4. Robert P. Lanza, Betsy L. Dresser, and Philip Damiani are optimistic that cloning will become an effective way to preserve endangered species. Ellen Goodman is not so hopeful, fearing that if habitat is not also preserved, cloning endangered species will be meaningless. Do you share Lanza's, Dresser's, and Damiani's optimism, or do you agree with Goodman that cloning endangered species alone is not enough to preserve a species? Explain, citing evidence from both viewpoints.

Chapter 2

1. Leon R. Kass argues that because they are only human, scientists can not be trusted with the god-like decisions that genetic engineering technology gives them. Michael Place is more optimistic about humankind and believes that genetic knowledge is a God-given gift that can be used to serve humanity. What predictions does each author make about how human beings will use genetic technology in the future? Which predictions do you find most persuasive? Explain your answer.

2. Megan Best bases her ethical opposition to cloning on the assumption that embryos are human beings and should not be created or sacrificed to benefit other human beings. Stuart K. Hayashi, on the other hand, rejects the assumption that the embryo is a human being. Is accepting or rejecting this assumption necessary to support each author's respective conclusions? Explain why or why not.

3. Which objections to genetically modified crops raised by the authors who oppose them in Chapter 3 does Gary Comstock address in his analysis? Could the same analysis be applied to the objections that he does not directly address? Citing from the text, explain why or why not.

Chapter 3

1. The authors in this chapter who support genetically engineered crops—L. Val Giddings, Jonathan Rauch, and Dennis T. Avery —often point to the fact that there is no scientific proof that GM crops are unsafe. The authors who oppose genetically engineered crops—John Grogan, Cheryl Long, and Ricarda Steinbrecher—argue that their side effects are uncertain, and that those who produce them must prove they are safe for consumers and the environment. What standard of proof do you think should be required before genetically engineered crops can be legally grown? Use quotes from the viewpoints while constructing your answer.

2. An oft-used argument made by those who oppose genetically engineered crops—such as John Grogan, Cheryl Long, and GeneWatch—is that a few multinational corporations own them. Because corporations are accountable to their stockholders, opponents argue, they are motivated by profit, not interest in public health. Do you agree or disagree with the claim that the profit motive of those who produce genetically engineered crops makes the safety of their products inherently suspect? Explain, supporting your position with evidence from the viewpoints.

3. Jonathan Rauch claims that genetically engineered crops are good for the environment because growing them is less harmful than traditional farming methods. Ricarda Steinbrecher argues that genetically engineered crops have unknown side effects that could damage the environment. Which do you think will have a greater adverse impact on the environment—the unknown side effects of genetically engineered crops or the loss of habitat to traditional farming? Explain.

Chapter 4

1. Y.G. Muralidharan argues that mandatory labeling of genetically engineered foods will help consumers make informed choices about the food they eat. Gregory Conko claims that negative labeling, labels that identify foods that contain no genetically modified organisms, are sufficient to inform consumers and will be less costly than mandatory labeling of genetically modified foods. Do you think negative labeling is sufficient to inform consumers? Explain, citing from the viewpoints.

2. Some commentators claim that the patenting of human genes discourages research because the monopoly created by the patent hinders further research that might produce better, less expensive products. David Holcberg maintains that the patenting of human genes rewards new discoveries and thus motivates research. While Holcberg stresses the need to reward research efforts directed at discovering new isolated genes, some analysts are concerned about discouraging subsequent research to improve its uses. Do you think these two views can be reconciled? Why or why not?

3. Robert A. Best claims that to avoid dealing with the issue that their experiments ultimately kill human embryos, scientists use other terms to describe these embryos, such as "unfertilized oocyte" and "clump of embryonic cells." What terms does Rudolf Jaenisch use when explaining why he opposes a ban on therapeutic cloning? Do you think he uses these terms to avoid addressing Best's concerns about killing embryos? What evidence in the viewpoint supports your conclusion?

Organizations to Contact

The editors have compiled the following list of organizations concerned with the issues debated in this book. The descriptions are derived from materials provided by the organizations. All have publications or information available for interested readers. The list was compiled on the date of publication of the present volume; names, addresses, and phone numbers may change. Be aware that many organizations take several weeks or longer to respond to inquiries, so allow as much time as possible.

Alliance for Bio-Integrity
2040 Pearl Ln., Fairfield, IA 52556
(641) 472-5554
e-mail: info@biointegrity.org • Web site: www.bio-integrity.org

The Alliance for Bio-Integrity is a nonprofit organization that opposes the use of genetic engineering in agriculture and works to educate the public about the dangers of genetically modified foods. Position papers that argue against genetic engineering from legal, religious, and scientific perspectives—including "Why Concerns About Health Risks of Genetically Engineered Food Are Scientifically Justified"—are available on its Web site.

Biotechnology Industry Organization (BIO)
1225 Eye St. NW, Suite 400, Washington, DC 20005
(202) 962-9200 • fax: (202) 962-9201
e-mail: biomember@bio.org • Web site: www.bio.org

BIO represents biotechnology companies, academic institutions, state biotechnology centers, and related organizations that support the use of biotechnology in improving health care, agriculture, efforts to clean up the environment, and other fields. BIO works to educate the public about biotechnology and respond to concerns about the safety of genetic engineering and other technologies. It publishes *Bioethics: Facing the Future Responsibly* and an introductory guide to biotechnology, which are available on its Web site.

Center for Bioethics and Human Dignity (CBHD)
2065 Half Day Rd., Bannockburn, IL 60015
(847) 317-8180 • fax: (847) 317-8153
e-mail: info@cbhd.org • Web site: www.cbhd.org

CBHD is an international education center whose purpose is to bring Christian perspectives to bear on contemporary bioethical challenges facing society. Its publications address genetic technologies as well as other topics such as euthanasia and abortion. It publishes the book *Cutting-Edge Bioethics* and the audio CD *The Challenges and Opportunities of Genetic Intervention.* The articles "Biotechnology's Brave New World" and "To Clone or Not to Clone?" are available on its Web site.

Coalition for the Advancement of Medical Research (CAMR)
2120 L St. NW, Suite 850, Washington, DC 20037
(202) 833-0355
e-mail: CAMResearch@yahoo.com
Web site: www.camradvocacy.org

CAMR is a coalition of nationally-recognized patient organizations, universities, scientific societies, foundations, and individuals with life-threatening illnesses and disorders, advocating for the advancement of breakthrough research and technologies in regenerative medicine, including stem cell research and somatic cell nuclear transfer, in order to cure disease and alleviate suffering. On its Web site, CAMR provides access to numerous articles on genetic technologies, including "Anti-Patent Legislation Could Cripple Medical Research" and "Stemming the Tide."

Council for Responsible Genetics (CRG)
5 Upland Rd., Suite 3, Cambridge, MA 02140
(617) 868-0870 • fax: (617) 491-5344
e-mail: crg@gene-watch.org • Web site: www.gene-watch.org

CRG is a national nonprofit organization of scientists, public health advocates, and others who promote a comprehensive public interest agenda for biotechnology. Its members work to raise public awareness about genetic discrimination, patenting life forms, food safety, and environmental quality. CRG publishes *GeneWatch* magazine, providing access to current and archived articles on its Web site.

Foundation on Economic Trends (FET)
1660 L St. NW, Suite 216, Washington, DC 20036
(202) 466-2823 • fax: (202) 429-9602
e-mail: office@foet.org • Web site: www.foet.org

Founded by science critic and author Jeremy Rifkin, the foundation is a nonprofit organization whose mission is to examine emerging trends in science and technology and their impacts on the environment, the economy, culture, and society. FET works to educate the public about topics such as gene patenting, commercial eugenics, genetic discrimination, and genetically altered food. Its Web site contains news updates and articles, including "Shopping for Humans" and "Unknown Risks of Genetically Engineered Crops."

Friends of the Earth (FOE)
1717 Massachusetts Ave. NW, Suite 600, Washington, DC
20036-2002
(877) 843-8687 • fax: (202) 783-0444
e-mail: foe@foe.org • Web site: www.foe.org
Founded in San Francisco in 1969 by David Brower, Friends of the
Earth is a grassroots organization whose goal is to create a more
healthy, just world. FOE members founded the world's largest federation of democratically elected environmental groups, Friends
of the Earth International. Among other efforts, FOE conducted
lab tests confirming that genetically engineered corn not approved
for human consumption was in products on supermarket shelves
across the nation. FOE publishes the quarterly newsmagazine
Friends of the Earth, current and archived issues of which are available on its Web site.

The Hastings Center
21 Malcolm Gordon Rd., Garrison, NY 10524-5555
(845) 424-4040 • fax: (845) 424-4545
e-mail: mail@thehastingscenter.org
Web site: www.thehastingscenter.org
The Hastings Center is an independent research institute that explores the medical, ethical, and social ramifications of biomedical
advances. The center publishes books, including *Reprogenetics*, the
bimonthly *Hastings Center Report*, and the bimonthly newsletter
IRB: Ethics & Human Research.

National Institutes of Health (NIH)
National Human Genome Research Institute (NHGRI)
9000 Rockville Pike, Bethesda, MD 20892
(301) 402-0911 • fax: (301) 402-2218
Web site: www.nhgri.nih.gov
NIH is the federal government's primary agency for the support of
biomedical research. As a division of NIH, NHGRI's mission was
to head the Human Genome Project, the federally funded effort to
map all human genes, which was completed in April 2003. Now,
NHGRI has moved into the genomic era with research aimed at
improving human health and fighting disease. Information on the
Project and relevant articles are available on its Web site.

Organic Consumers Association (OCA)
6101 Cliff Estate Rd., Little Marais, MN 55614
(218) 226-4164 • fax: (218) 353-7652
Web site: www.organicconsumers.org

The OCA promotes food safety, organic farming, and sustainable agriculture practices. It provides information on the hazards of genetically engineered food, irradiated food, food grown with toxic sludge fertilizer, mad cow disease, rBGH in milk, and other issues, and organizes boycotts and protests around these issues. It publishes *BioDemocracy News* and its Web site includes many fact sheets and articles on genetically modified foods.

Patients' Coalition for Urgent Research (CURe)
Alliance for Aging Research
2021 K St. NW, Suite 305, Washington, DC 20006
(202) 293-2856 • fax: (202) 785-8574
Web site: www.agingresearch.org

CURe is a coalition of more than thirty patient advocacy and disease groups, under the leadership of the Alliance for Aging Research, actively lobbying for federal funding for embryo and stem cell research. CURe believes that science can help people live longer, more productive lives.

President's Council on Bioethics
1801 Pennsylvania Ave. NW, Suite 700, Washington, DC 20006
(202) 296-4669
e-mail: info@bioethics.gov • Web site: www.bioethics.gov

When the National Bioethics Advisory Commission's charter expired in October 2001, President George W. Bush established the President's Council on Bioethics. It works to protect the rights and welfare of human research subjects and govern the management and use of genetic information. On its Web site, the council provides access to its reports "Human Cloning and Human Dignity: An Ethical Inquiry" and "Beyond Therapy: Biotechnology and the Pursuit of Happiness."

Stanford University Center for Biomedical Ethics (SCBE)
701 Welch Rd., Bldg. A, Suite 1105, Palo Alto, CA 94304
(650) 723-5760 • fax: (650) 725-6131
e-mail: SCBE-info@med.stanford.edu
Web site: http://scbe.stanford.edu

SCBE engages in interdisciplinary research on moral questions arising from the complex relationships among medicine, science, and society. The center is committed to exploring and promoting compassionate approaches to the practice of medicine in a climate of socioeconomic and technological change. SCBE publishes the newsletter *Stanford Bioethics*, recent issues of which are available on its Web site.

U.S. Department of Agriculture (USDA)

14th & Independence Ave. SW, Washington, DC 20250
Web site: www.nal.usda.gov/bic

The USDA is one of three federal agencies, along with the Environmental Protection Agency (EPA) and the U.S. Food and Drug Administration (FDA), primarily responsible for regulating biotechnology in the United States. The USDA conducts research on the safety of genetically engineered organisms, helps form government policy on agricultural biotechnology, and provides information to the public about these technologies.

Additional Internet Resources

The following Internet resources may be useful to students interested in learning more about genetic engineering.

BetterHumans.com

www.betterhumans.com

BetterHumans.com explores and advocates the use of science and technology for furthering human progress.

Genetically Engineered Organisms Public Issues Education Project (GEO-PIE)

www.geo-pie.cornell.edu/gmo.html

The GEO-PIE Project was developed to create objective educational materials exploring the complex scientific and social issues associated with genetic engineering in order to help readers consider those issues for themselves.

Germline.net

www.germline.net

The Web site, created by Dr. Nelson Erlick, author of *Germline*, has many useful links to other Web sites and articles concerning gene therapy and genetics.

HumanCloning.org

www.humancloning.org

HumanCloning.org promotes education about human cloning and other forms of biotechnology and emphasizes the positive aspects of these technologies. The Web site contains numerous fact sheets and articles on the benefits of human cloning, including "In Support of the Argument for Human Cloning."

Bibliography of Books

Britt Bailey and Marc Lappé, eds.	*Engineering the Farm: Ethical and Social Aspects of Agricultural Biotechnology.* Washington, DC: Island Press, 2002.
Finn Bowring	*Science, Seeds, and Cyborgs: Biotechnology and the Appropriation of Life.* New York: Verso, 2003.
Allen Buchanan	*From Chance to Choice: Genetics and Justice.* New York: Cambridge University Press, 2000.
Audrey R. Chapman and Mark S. Frankel, eds.	*Designing Our Descendants: The Promises and Perils of Genetic Modification.* Baltimore, MD: Johns Hopkins University Press, 2003.
Daniel Charles	*Lords of the Harvest: Biotech, Big Money, and the Future of Food.* Cambridge, MA: Perseus, 2001.
Ronald Cole-Turner	*Beyond Cloning: Religion and the Remaking of Humanity.* Harrisburg, PA: Trinity Press International, 2003.
Ronnie Cummins	*Genetically Engineered Food: A Self-Defense Guide for Consumers.* New York: Marlowe, 2000.
Celia Deane-Drummond and Bronislaw Szerszynski	*Reordering Nature: Theology, Society, and the New Genetics.* London: T & T Clark, 2003.
Timothy J. Demy and Gary P. Stewart, eds.	*Genetic Engineering: A Christian Response.* Grand Rapids, MI: Kregel, 1999.
John Hyde Evans	*Playing God?: Human Genetic Engineering and the Rationalization of Public Bioethical Debate.* Chicago: University of Chicago Press, 2002.
Michael W. Fox	*Beyond Evolution: The Genetically Altered Future of Plants, Animals, the Earth, and Humans.* New York: Lyons, 1999.
Francis Fukuyama	*Our Posthuman Future: Consequences of the Biotechnology Revolution.* New York: Farrar, Straus, and Giroux, 2002.
Hille Haker and Deryck Beyleveld, eds.	*The Ethics of Genetics in Human Procreation.* Aldershot, UK: Ashgate, 2000.
Bill Lambrecht	*Dinner at the New Gene Café: How Genetic Engineering Is Changing What We Eat, How We Live, and the Global Politics of Food.* New York: Thomas Dunne Books, 2001.
Paul F. Lurquin	*High Tech Harvest: Understanding Genetically Modified Food Plants.* Boulder, CO: Westview Press, 2002.

David Magnus and Alva Butcher, eds.   *Contemporary Genetic Technology: Scientific, Ethical, and Social Challenges.* Melbourne, FL: Krieger, 2000.

David Magnus, Arthur Caplan, and Glenn McGee, eds.   *Who Owns Life?* Amherst, NY: Prometheus Books, 2002.

Glenn McGee   *The Perfect Baby: Parenthood in the New World of Cloning and Genetics.* Lanham, MD: Rowman & Littlefield, 2000.

Alan McHughen   *Pandora's Picnic Basket: The Potential and Hazards of Genetically Modified Foods.* New York: Oxford University Press, 2000.

Stephen Nottingham   *Eat Your Genes: How Genetically Modified Food Is Entering Our Diet.* New York: Zed Books, 2003.

Per Pinstrup-Andersen and Ebbe Schiøler   *Seeds of Contention: World Hunger and the Global Controversy over GM Crops.* Baltimore, MD: Johns Hopkins University Press, 2000.

Jonathon Porritt   *Playing Safe: Science and the Environment.* London: Thames & Hudson, 2000.

Derrick A. Purdue   *Anti-GenetiX: The Emergence of the Anti-GM Movement.* Aldershot, UK: Ashgate, 2000.

Gregory Stock   *Redesigning Humans: Our Inevitable Genetic Future.* Boston: Houghton Mifflin, 2002.

Gregory Stock and John Campbell   *Engineering the Human Germline: An Exploration of the Science and Ethics of Altering the Genes We Pass to Our Children.* New York: Oxford University Press, 2000.

Martin Teitel and Kimberly A. Wilson   *Genetically Engineered Food: Changing the Nature of Nature.* Rochester, VT: Park Street Press, 2001.

Brian Tokar, ed.   *Redesigning Life?: The Worldwide Challenge to Genetic Engineering.* New York: Zed Books, 2001.

Index

217

Law, Medicine and Ethics Program (Boston University Schools of Medicine and Public Health), 82
Levine, Judith, 55
Long, Cheryl, 126
Louis XV (king of France), 171
L-tryptophan, 33–34

Mahowald, Mary, 61
maize, 167, 182, 183
malnutrition, 165
mammoth, 73
"Manifesto for Cyborgs: Science, Technology, and Socialist Feminism in the 1980s, A" (Haraway), 64
medicines, 21, 22, 24–25
meningitis, 133
mental illness, 19
Mexico, 28, 149, 160, 163, 167
  drought in, 30
mice, 50, 57, 195
Midas, 89–90
Midgley, Mary, 117–18
milk, 7, 25, 27, 132, 162
Miller, Henry I., 21
monarch butterflies, 130–31, 134, 139–40
Monsanto, 127, 130, 145, 155, 167
  efforts of, to patent genes, 36
  herbicide-tolerant cotton and, 157
moral issues, 42, 90, 98, 187–89
  Catholic-Christian perspective on, 92–97
  commodification of life and, 32, 45–46, 117, 191
  designer baby theory and, 20, 43, 61, 86–87, 191
  fallacy of, 64–65
  genetically modified foods and, 111–12, 115, 120, 132
  issue of humans "playing God" and, 85, 110, 113–14, 171
  naïve consequentialism and, 118
  religion versus ethics in, 116, 119
  see also human dignity
Muralidharan, Y.G., 173

National Academy of Sciences, U.S., 24, 49
National Bioethics Advisory Commission, 88, 197
National Institutes of Health, 27
National Women's Health Network, 60
naturalism, 64
Nature (journal), 48
Nazis, 22, 37, 57, 186, 187
New England Journal of Medicine (NEJM), 132

Newman, Stuart, 57–58
New Scientist (magazine), 131
New York Medical College, 57
New York Times (newspaper), 57, 192
New York Times Magazine, 30, 82
New Zealand, 176
Nobel Peace Prize, 148, 171
Norsigian, Judy, 56
Nova (TV series), 56
Nuremburg Code, 57, 185, 186

oil spill cleanup, 24, 127
O'Reilly, Brian, 124
organ harvesting, 41, 88, 89, 118, 196–97
Organic Consumers Association, 32
Organic Gardening (magazine), 126, 127, 133
Organization for Economic Co-operation and Development (OECD), 153
Orissa (India), 30

Packaged Commodity Rules, 179
Parkinson's disease, 51, 172, 193, 195, 196
Pakistan, 148
Pasteur, Louis, 198, 199
Patent and Trademark Office (PTO), 199–201
Patent Office (UK), 44, 45
patents, 32, 36, 45, 126, 167
  biotech companies' rush to own, 35–37, 43
  scientists should be allowed to own, 198–201
penicillin, 23
pesticides, 14, 143, 147, 160, 162
  benefits of gene-spliced crops and, 25
  problems of gene-spliced crops and, 129–30, 155–57
pharmacogenetics, 93
Philippines, 148
Pinstrup-Anderson, Per, 161
Pioneer Hi-Bred International, 132
Place, Michael, 92
Plant Genetics Systems, 124
ploughing, 145
Pollan, Michael, 30
Pope, Charles Earle, 72
population growth, 78, 144, 150, 165
poverty, 164, 165, 166
President's Council on Bioethics, 84
Prevention of Food Adulteration Act (India), 176, 179
privacy, 36, 37
Program on Medicine, Technology, and Society (UCLA), 83

221